The SCREAMING HAIRY ARMADILLO

and 76 Other Animals with Weird, Wild Names

MATTHEW MURRIE and **STEVE MURRIE**
illustrated by **JULIE BENBASSAT**

WORKMAN PUBLISHING ★ NEW YORK

Library of Congress Cataloging-in-Publication Data is available.

ISBN 978-1-5235-0811-2

Design by Sara Corbett and Lisa Hollander
Photo research by Sophia Rieth

Workman books are available at special discounts when purchased in bulk for premiums and sales promotions as well as for fund-raising or educational use. Special editions or book excerpts can also be created to specification. For details, contact the Special Sales Director at the address below, or send an email to specialmarkets@workman.com.

Workman Publishing Company, Inc.
225 Varick Street
New York, NY 10014-4381
workman.com

Workman is a registered trademark of Workman Publishing Co., Inc.

Printed in China

First printing May 2020

10 9 8 7 6 5 4 3 2 1

CONTENTS

2 MAGICAL NAMES

3 FIERCE NAMES

WHAT'S IN A NAME?

Imagine a world where nobody has a name. How would you know when someone is addressing you? How would you refer to people who weren't around? How would you talk about your favorite musician, sports player, or fictional character?

Names help us distinguish between people and make it easy for us to refer to one another. If you and I have a friend named Tim, we can have a conversation about Tim and be sure we're talking about the same person by using his name. If Tim *didn't* have a name, we might have to try to describe him. "You know, our tall friend with the short hair?" Things could get pretty confusing pretty fast!

Names often become part of our identity, as well. Sharing our name is a way of expressing ourselves to the world, and it helps us stand out as individuals.

Well, just like *you* need a name, animals need names, too. And we're not just talking about a pet name like Fido or Rocky or Mr. Mittens. Animal species need names so that we can distinguish between them and talk about them easily.

It's a lot like you and me talking about our friend Tim: When you say "dog," you can be sure that whoever you're talking to will picture a dog. But if dogs didn't have a name—if you called them "those four-legged things"—someone might think you're talking about cats, or pigs, or horses!

Four-legged things

The ability to refer to animals accurately is especially important for the scientists who study them—and often, scientists are the ones who come up with species names.

Now, scientists have a reputation for being a little dry. But when it comes to naming animals, it turns out they can be pretty creative, expressive, and downright silly!

HOW DO SCIENTISTS NAME ANIMALS?

Have you ever named a pet? Perhaps a dog, a cat, a hamster, or a goldfish? How did you come up with its name? Maybe you chose a name that described its physical features, such as its color, size, or shape. Maybe you based the name on its movement or behavior—the way it runs, jumps, splashes, or squeals (if your dog follows you around everywhere, perhaps you named her Shadow!). Or maybe you named your pet after your favorite superhero, cartoon character, famous person, or even a friend or relative.

Scientists come up with animal species names the same way. Some animals are named for a unique physical feature. For example, the horned lizard is named for—you guessed it—the horns that protrude from its head. Other animals are named for their behavior. Killer whales aren't actually whales; they're dolphins. But they do kill whales! They were originally referred to as "whale killers," which morphed over time into "killer whales."

Horned lizard

But animals aren't always named for their appearance or behavior. Many scientists love to reference their favorite fictional characters—Batman fan Pablo Lehmann Albornoz named a catfish *Otocinclus batmani*, while paleontologist Samuel Turvey named an extinct marine animal *Han solo* after the Star Wars hero. And some scientists just love a good joke, like Paul Marsh, who named a wasp *Heerz lukenatcha* (say it out loud!).

You might have noticed that some animal names are easy to say, like killer whale, while others are longer, harder to say, and in *italics*, like *Otocinclus batmani*. That's because most animals actually have two names—a **scientific name** (that's the long, hard-to-say, *italic* one) and a **common name** (the easy one).

THE SCOOP ON SCIENTIFIC NAMES

While, technically, anyone can name an animal, special scientists called taxonomists specialize in naming and classifying organisms (**organism** is just a fancy word for something that's alive). **Taxonomy** is the science of defining and naming organisms based on what they have in common with each other. Each organism gets sorted into groups called taxa, with a single group called a taxon. There are eight taxa—domain, kingdom, phylum, class, order, family, genus, and species—with the highest-ranking taxon (domain) being the broadest and the lowest (species) being the most specific.

This can get a little confusing, so let's break it down by looking at how the domestic cat is classified. Regardless of whether it's a tabby, a tuxedo cat, or a hairless Sphynx, scientifically speaking, your favorite whisker-sporting feline is classified like this:

Meow

DOMAIN: Eukarya
KINGDOM: Animalia
PHYLUM: Chordata
CLASS: Mammalia
ORDER: Carnivora
FAMILY: Felidae
GENUS: Felis
SPECIES: Felis catus

What does this tell us? Well, cats belong to the **Eukarya** domain, which includes all the organisms in the world whose cells have a nucleus surrounded by a membrane. Getting a little more specific, they fall into the Animalia kingdom, which includes all the world's animals. Next, they get sorted into the Chordata phylum, which is a more specific group of animals that all have certain features, like a circulatory system.

As you can see, each taxon gets more and more specific. By the time we get to genus, things are pretty specific indeed—the *Felis* genus only includes domestic cats and some of their bigger relatives, such as wildcats and jungle cats. Finally, there's the species, *Felis catus*, which refers specifically to the domestic cat. So, *Felis catus* is the scientific name for cats.

What about human beings?

DOMAIN:	Eukarya
KINGDOM:	Animalia
PHYLUM:	Chordata
CLASS:	Mammalia
ORDER:	Primates
FAMILY:	Hominidae
GENUS:	Homo
SPECIES:	Homo sapiens

As you can see, humans and cats belong to the same domain, kingdom, phylum, and class. When we get to order, though, we start branching in different directions—humans belong to the Primates order, which also includes monkeys, apes, and lemurs; cats, however, belong to the Carnivora order, along with dogs, bears, and lots of other meat-eating mammals. As with cats, each taxon gets more and more specific, until we finally get to the species name (aka the scientific name) for humans: *Homo sapiens*. This refers to humans and only humans!

To come up with scientific names like *Felis catus* and *Homo sapiens*, scientists use a two-term naming system called **binomial nomenclature**, which was developed by an eighteenth-century Swedish botanist named Carl Linnaeus. The first name in the binomial identifies which genus the organism belongs to and the second name specifies the exact species within that genus. Both parts of the name are based in Latin grammatical forms, but this does not mean they have to be Latin in origin. They just have to sound Latin (like *Otocinclus batmani*!).

These Latin or Latin-ish names can be pretty hard to say, though. So, in addition to a scientific name, many organisms also have common names.

CRAZY COMMON NAMES

A common name is what most people use when referring to an animal. For example, you probably call it a cat, not a *Felis catus*.

Common names are often more creative and funnier than scientific names. Case in point: The bird species scientifically known as *Cephalopterus penduliger* is also called

XVII

the long-wattled umbrellabird (page 2)! Sometimes scientists come up with these common names, but sometimes ordinary people do. And some animals have lots of common names, kind of like nicknames—the hellbender (page 64) is also called the snot otter, the lasagna lizard, and the devil dog! That's why it's important for each animal to also have a scientific name—however many common names an animal might have, scientists can use its fancy scientific name and be sure they are talking about the right creature.

This book will focus mostly on common names, but keep an eye out for some wacky scientific names, as well! (Who's hungry for some *Pieza pi*? See page 112!)

ARE YOU READY?

Prepare yourself. You are about to meet some of the strangest—and strangest-named—creatures on the planet. From the sparklemuffin peacock spider (page 7) to the bone-eating snot flower worm (page 74), these animals will make you gasp, laugh, and marvel at their wild names and just-as-wild behavior.

By the time you're done, you might be ready to start coming up with your own animal names. Luckily, there's a handy Weird and Wild Name Generator at the back of the book to help you do just that!

FUNNY NAMES

1

HA HA HA HA!

HA HA HA!!

Some scientists have quite the sense of humor when it comes to naming the animals they discover. In this chapter, you will meet creatures with downright silly names, from the **SARCASTIC FRINGEHEAD** and the **SPARKLEMUFFIN PEACOCK SPIDER** to the **SMOOTH-HEADED BLOBFISH** and the **BLUE-FOOTED BOOBY** (yes, these are all real names!).

Along the way, you'll learn all about the hilarious things these animals do to earn their wacky monikers. Because however much fun scientists might have deciding what to call animals, there is usually a method to their madness—a clear, scientific connection between the name and a characteristic of the creature.

So get ready: You're about to come face-to-face with animals that are as laugh-out-loud unique as their unbelievable names!

LONG-WATTLED

The male umbrellabird's wattle can be over 18 inches long!

Wattle

You can probably guess where the "umbrella" in this bird's common name comes from—just look at that crest on its head! It's like this bird has its own built-in rain shield! But what on earth is a wattle?

A wattle is a type of **caruncle.** The word "caruncle" comes from the Latin term for flesh, *caruncula,* so scientists today call any fleshy part hanging on a bird a caruncle. There are several different and weird-sounding types of caruncles in addition to a wattle, like a dewlap and a snood.

2

UMBRELLA-BIRD

Caruncles are found around the head, neck, throat, or eyes of a bird.

As you can tell by its name, the umbrellabird's caruncle is a rather long wattle hanging down from its throat. The wattle amplifies the male umbrellabird's voice when he sings to impress the females. (Only male umbrellabirds have long wattles. Females have short wattles or no wattles at all.)

But wait . . . How do the males fly with such a long wattle? The long-wattled umbrellabird has full control over his wattle, blowing it out when it is time to sing and pulling it in when it is time to fly. Still, these birds are not the best flyers, so they tend to hop from branch to branch instead of soaring.

SPECIES: *Cephalopterus penduliger*

HABITAT: The wet mountain forests along the coast of Colombia and Ecuador

"PICK ME!" Female umbrellabirds are very selective, which means the males really have to work to win them over!

A female umbrellabird

SARCASTIC FRINGEHEAD

Considering this fish's common name, you would be forgiven for thinking it has a snarky sense of humor. After all, that's what we usually mean when we use the word "sarcastic" nowadays.

But like many words, the meaning of "sarcastic" has changed over time. It comes from the Greek word *sarkazein*, which originally meant "to tear flesh like a dog." Over time, the word expanded to include less violent meanings like "to bite one's lip in rage," "to gnash one's teeth," and eventually "to sneer." Finally, it came to mean what it does today: a manner of speaking characterized by biting words.

The sarcastic fringehead's name recalls the original meaning of *sarkazein*—because while this fish might not make any snarky remarks,

SPECIES: *Neoclinus blanchardi*

HABITAT: The Pacific Ocean along the west coast of Mexico and the United States

YIKES! Sarcastic fringeheads have been known to attack divers.

5

See the fringe?

it does have a ferocious, flesh-tearing bite! Its mouth is a whopping four times larger open than closed. Yikes! Even better, it's lined with razor-sharp, spiny teeth, which come in handy when the male sarcastic fringehead is guarding his **burrow** (a burrow is a hole that an animal lives in).

It's the job of the male to protect the eggs of female fringeheads—and boy, do these fish protect those eggs! If anything comes too close to their brood, or if the sarcastic fringeheads are just feeling a bit peckish, CHOMP!

Those teeth help settle territory disputes, too. When one sarcastic fringehead invades the turf of another, they both open their mouths as wide as possible to engage in a "lip-lock." In other words, they wrestle with their mouths!

As for the "fringehead" in this fish's name, look no further than the fringe of **cirri** (thin, hair-like structures that look like tiny tentacles) on its face.

SPARKLE-MUFFIN
PEACOCK SPIDER

Has a very sparkly backside

Like peacocks, it proudly displays its colors to attract a mate

When you are assigned a scientific name like *Maratus jactatus*, your common name could use a little sparkle. The sparklemuffin peacock spider was named by biologist Madeline Girard, who discovered it in 2014 while searching for peacock spiders in Australia.

All spiders in the genus *Maratus* are commonly called peacock spiders. The name is a no-brainer—the male spiders in this genus all come equipped with brightly colored backsides that flip up to impress female peacock spiders.

The award for most impressive peacock spider backside, though, probably belongs to the sparklemuffin. This flashy spider looks like it's dragging around a muffin that was dipped in a magic rainbow!

Like all peacock spiders, the sparklemuffin belongs to the Salticidae family of jumping spiders. Instead of spinning webs to catch food, these arachnids use

SPECIES: *Maratus jactatus*

HABITAT: *Australia*

YOUR TURN! Think of an animal with a really simple or boring name, like cat, dog, or pig. Come up with a new, more sparkly name for this creature based on its color, shape, or personality!

8

their excellent eyesight to hunt down prey before jumping on them and delivering a venom-filled bite. (We don't have to worry, luckily—jumping spiders are too tiny to carry enough venom to harm humans!)

Peacock spiders don't just use their legs for jumping, however. They are also renowned dancers. Male spiders perform elaborate dance moves to woo any lady spiders they spot jumping by. The dances are truly something to behold—as the spiders wave their legs through the air, they look like traffic conductors who have had a bit too much coffee.

And if a male's dance isn't up to the lady spider's standards? There's a good chance he will need to use those legs to jump away, because females often try to eat male dancers that disappoint them!

Lift your arms and dance like a peacock spider!

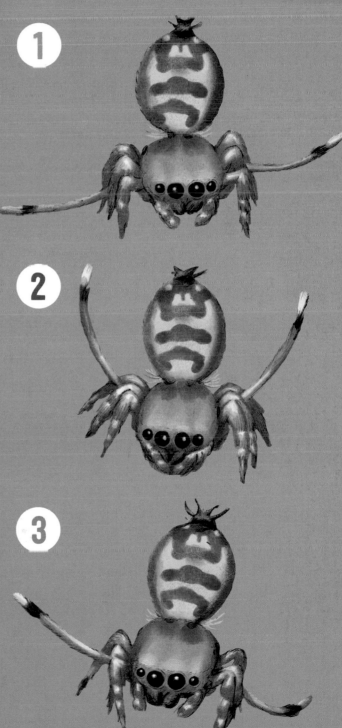

1

2

3

A PEACOCK

While the sparklemuffin might be the most eye-catching of the peacock spiders, it's not the only one with style. Meet these other four fabulous peacock spiders who love to flash their sometimes spooky but always spectacular backsides!

SKELETORUS *(Maratus sceletus)* With its skeleton-like pattern, this peacock spider looks like it's all dressed up for Halloween. But those spooky markings serve another purpose: impressing the female spiders. When a male skeletorus spots a female he'd like to get to know, he inflates his **spinneret** (a silk-producing organ) and raises his tail.

BURNT-ORANGE PEACOCK SPIDER

(Maratus combustus) This peacock spider gets its scientific species name (*combustus* is Latin for "burn up") and common name ("burnt-orange") from the flame color of the male's abdomen. It was first discovered trying to stoke the hearts of female peacock spiders on Mount Romance in Australia.

SPIDER ROUNDUP

KITTY-CAT PEACOCK SPIDER *(Maratus felinus)*

Like many great discoveries, the kitty-cat peacock spider was found purely by accident. Australian biologist Joseph Strubert discovered this species while looking at photographs of what he thought were other peacock spiders. Upon closer examination, he started noticing some differences—including a pattern in the shape of a cat's face on the spider's abdomen!

EAGLE PEACOCK SPIDER *(Maratus aquilus)*

The eagle peacock spider gets its common name and its scientific name (*aquila* is Latin for "eagle") thanks to its eagle-shaped pattern. It also calls Mount Romance home, although its habitat does not overlap with the burnt-orange peacock spider.

SOUTHERN HAIRY-NOSED WOMBAT

Not a bat!

What's the opposite of a bare-nosed wombat? A hairy-nosed wombat, of course!

If you're thinking a wombat is a kind of bat, think again: Wombats are Australian **marsupials**, like kangaroos. Also like 'roos, wombats carry their babies, called **joeys**, in pouches (those pouches are what makes a marsupial a marsupial). However, unlike a kangaroo's forward-facing pouch, the opening of a wombat's pouch faces rearward. This way, wombats don't get dirt in their pouches while digging their **burrows**.

And wombats love to dig! In fact, they are natural-born digging machines, earning the nickname "bulldozers of the bush"

SPECIES: *Lasiorhinus latifrons*

HABITAT: Southern coast of Australia

CUBED CACA: Wombat droppings are cube-shaped! Why? Scientists believe the distinct shape of a wombat's intestines give form to its poop.

12

(in Australia, **bush** refers to rural, forested land). With their powerful forearms and strong, well-clawed paws, wombats dig huge systems of interconnected burrows.

There are three species of wombat, all native to Australia: the bare-nosed wombat, the northern hairy-nosed wombat, and the southern hairy-nosed wombat. The hairy-nosed wombats are distinguished by— you guessed it—their very hairy snouts. While southern hairy-nosed wombats can be found digging burrows along the southern coast of Australia, the critically endangered northern hairy-nosed wombats all live in the state of Queensland. (A **critically endangered species** has a very low population in the wild and is at risk of extinction. To find out more about endangered animals, see page 154.)

STRIPED PYJAMA SQUID

When it comes to pyjamas, are you a stripes or polka-dot person? The *Sepioloidea lineolata* is stripes all the way. This creature's common name is a misnomer, however—while its pattern might look like fashionable jammies, it doesn't actually wear pyjamas, or even sleep at night.

If you haven't rubbed the sleep out of your eyes, you might have trouble seeing the striped pyjama squid. Growing to only about 2 inches long, it is teeny-tiny, and you probably won't spot one during the day—it's **nocturnal**, meaning it sleeps during the day and is active at night.

Cuttlefish? More like "cuddle-fish!"

14

The striped pyjama squid spends most of the day resting beneath the surface of the seafloor. During the night, it peeks out occasionally to grab a bite of fish or shrimp with its feeding tentacles, which are complete with suckers to help this tiny **cephalopod** capture its prey. (Sea creatures that have either arms or tentacles, including squids and octopuses, belong to the class Cephalopoda and are called cephalopods.)

Although the striped pyjama squid has two long feeding tentacles and eight other arms, just like other squids, it's actually not a squid at all—it's a cuttlefish. While squids and cuttlefish are both members of the class Cephalopoda, they fall into different orders based on their shape. Squids have a sleeker, more elongated look, while cuttlefish tend to be stubbier and stouter.

In case you're thinking about throwing a pyjama party with this cuttlefish, be warned: The striped pyjama squid can be a real party pooper. When it believes it is in danger, it oozes out poisonous slime!

SPECIES: *Sepioloidea lineolata*

HABITAT: The Indo–Pacific waters south of Australia

MASTER OF DISGUISE: Those striped pyjamas aren't just a fashion statement—they also help this critter conceal itself among seashells and other objects in its environment.

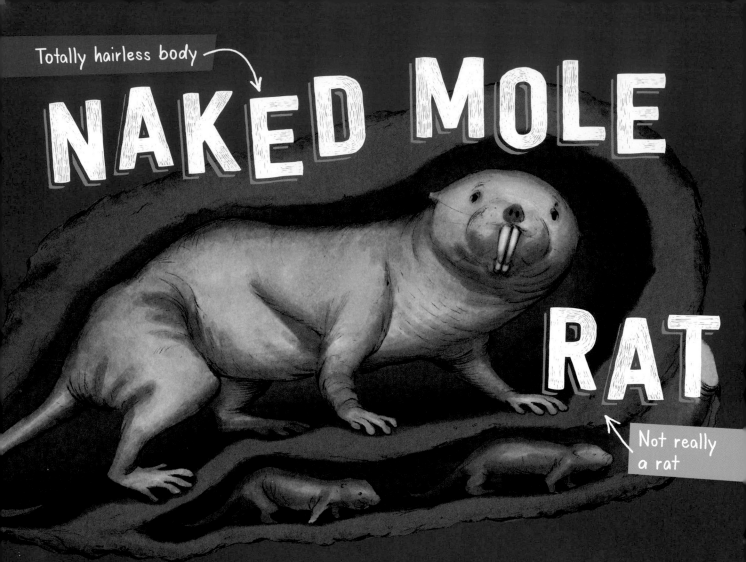

NAKED MOLE RAT

Not really a rat

T he only thing scientists got right when they named the naked mole rat is that it's naked. It's true: This bucktoothed creature is totally nude, with hairless, wrinkly, pink skin covering its mouse-size body. But technically, it's not a mole or even a rat! Despite its rat-like tail, the naked mole rat's nearest relatives are actually chinchillas, porcupines, and guinea pigs. As the only member of the Heterocephalidae family, the naked mole rat is truly a one-of-a-kind rodent.

16

Because naked mole rats live in the hot deserts of East Africa, they don't need fur. At night when it gets cool, naked mole rats crowd together to keep warm. And considering that a colony of naked mole rats consists of up to three hundred of these nude critters, it must not be too hard to get cozy!

Naked mole rats are tunnel dwellers.

Naked mole rats dwell in underground tunnel systems as large as six football fields, and these tunnels are complex—a single system will have special chambers similar to a human's house. Some chambers are for nesting mothers, some are storage areas for food, and some serve as indoor toilets, so naked mole rats don't have to venture outside when it's time to pee or poop.

Their sharp buckteeth are strong enough to bore through concrete and come in handy for eating the tough underground roots and tubers they call food. Think that's rough? Get ready to digest what's next: They also eat their own poop! Naked mole rats have adapted to be able to digest additional nutrients from the same food the second time around. Now, that's recycling!

SPECIES: *Heterocephalus glaber*

HABITAT: Deserts of East Africa

THANK YOU, NAKED MOLE RATS!
Naked mole rats have a chemical called **hyaluronan** in their bodies that blocks the formation of cancer tumors. As a result, these rats can live a lot longer than their rodent relatives. Scientists studying hyaluronan in naked mole rats believe what they discover may help fight cancer and aging in humans, too.

17

Why have one common name when you can have two? The monkeyface prickleback is also known as the monkeyface eel, and it's easy to see why—it looks like an eel with the face of a monkey!

It's not actually a monkey, of course, and it's not a true eel, either. Instead, it's a prickleback, another name for a fish in the family Stichaeidae. Fish in this family typically have tiny spines running along the **dorsal fin** on their back, hence the "prickleback."

Its scientific name, *Cebidicthys violaceus*, is just as fitting. *Cebidicthys* is a combination of the Latin word *cebidae*, the scientific name for a family of monkeys, and *icthys*, the Greek word for "fish." *Violaceus* is Latin for "violet," another word for purple (monkey faces sport various colorations, and some have purple hues). Put them all together and you have a violet monkey fish. That's a pretty great name, too!

Whatever you call them, these unusual sea creatures pass their days searching for algae and **crustaceans** (animals like shrimp, lobsters, and crabs) to munch on, while trying to avoid becoming lunch for giant egrets or other **piscivorous** (fish-eating) birds flying over the waves.

SPECIES: *Cebidichthys violaceus*

HABITAT: The monkeyface prickleback is a neritic (coastal) fish and can be found near the shores of Oregon in the United States all the way down to the Mexican state of Baja California.

A FISH OUT OF WATER: Monkeyface pricklebacks can breathe air for up to 35 hours out of water, as long as they are kept moist.

CUCKOO WASP

When you hear the word "cuckoo," what comes to mind? Something crazy, silly, bizarre, or weird? That's usually what we mean by "cuckoo," but when it comes to the animal world, "cuckoo" can mean smart, crafty, and deceptive. For example, the cuckoo bird lays its eggs in the nests of other birds, leaving the unsuspecting nest builders to feed and care for the cuckoo's offspring.

The cuckoo wasp has a similar M.O. (modus operandi), laying its eggs in the nests of solitary bees and wasps. The cuckoo wasp **larvae** (worm-like babies that will later transform into adult wasps) feed on the larvae of the host wasp, sometimes even kicking out the host's larvae so that the baby cuckoos can have all the food the host brings to the nest. Now, that's crafty!

Since the hosts have strong **mandibles** (jaws) and/or stingers, the

cuckoo wasp has developed a thick **exoskeleton** (a hard outer layer that covers and protects the body). The exoskeleton is flexible enough to allow the cuckoo wasp to roll up into a protective ball when threatened. This process of curling up into a defensive ball is called **conglobation** and is also seen in armadillos and pill bugs.

One might think of cuckoo wasps as **parasites** (organisms that survive by taking resources from another organism), but scientists classify them as **parasitoids** because they kill and feed on their host's offspring. Since they steal the food meant for the host's offspring, they are also considered **kleptoparasites** (thief parasites).

With all that killing and stealing, you might be wondering if there's anything redeeming about the cuckoo wasp. Look no further than their magnificent, metallically colored bodies with shimmering iridescent blues, purples, and greens that rival the colors of a peacock's tail feathers!

SPECIES: *Chrysis ignita*

HABITAT: Throughout the world

SO MANY CUCKOOS! There are more than three thousand species of cuckoo wasps.

A WORLD OF

When it comes to curiously named wasps, cuckoos are just the beginning. From puns to Harry Potter references, these four wasps prove that any name is fair game!

DEMENTOR WASP

(*Ampulex dementor*) Visitors at the Berlin Museum of Natural History got to choose this wasp's name, a reference to those soul-sucking monsters from J. K. Rowling's Harry Potter books. Dementor wasps prey on cockroaches in the most gruesome way imaginable: They sting the roach with their venomous stingers and then inject their eggs into the roach. When the eggs hatch, the wasp **larvae** eat the roach from the inside out!

AHA HA

When **entomologist** (a scientist who studies insects) Arnold Menke discovered this species of Australian wasp in 1977, he realized he had discovered not only a new wasp but also a new genus. He quite naturally exclaimed, "aha!" And the name stuck!

22

WASPS

HEERZ LUKENATCHA AND *HEERZ TOOYA*

Here's to you, Paul Marsh, and every other scientist with a sense of humor! In another life, Marsh might have been a comedian. He named two species of wasps under the genus *Heerz*: *Heerz lukenatcha* and *Heerz tooya*. (Say them out loud!)

LUSIUS MALFOYI

The Dementor isn't the only wasp named after a J. K. Rowling character. When Tom Saunders got the chance to name one of the three thousand wasps that call New Zealand home, he chose *Lusius malfoyi*, a reference to the villainous Lucius Malfoy. However, it wasn't Lucius's nastiness that Saunders wanted to associate with the wasp; it was his redemption. (No spoilers here—you'll have to read the Harry Potter series to understand why Malfoy deserves redemption!) Saunders hopes the name will raise awareness that, despite their nasty reputation, most wasps don't have stingers and don't pose any threats to humans.

23

BA HUMBUGI

Say it out loud!

A reference to *A Christmas Carol*

WACKY SCIENTIFIC NAME ALERT!

Who says scientists are a bunch of scrooges? When **malacologist** (a scientist who studies **mollusks**) Alan Solem discovered this tiny land snail under a log on the Fijian island of Viti Levu, he decided to have a little fun with the naming.

Solem didn't just discover a new species, but a new genus, as well. After naming the genus *Ba* for the Mba District of Viti Levu where he found the snail, Solem couldn't resist the urge to give it the *humbugi* species name. Say it out loud: *Ba humbugi.* You probably sound like Ebenezer Scrooge, the cranky old man in *A Christmas Carol* who loves to say "bah humbug!"

The yellowish-white *Ba humbugi* is an incredibly small snail with a shell that grows to only 0.09 to 0.13 inches in diameter. No wonder the four *Ba humbugi* specimens Solem studied are still the only four known to exist!

Ba humbugi may be one of the smallest and rarest mollusks on the planet, but it's a part of one of the most populated phyla in the animal kingdom: Mollusca. The members of Mollusca, known as mollusks, are all **invertebrates** with soft bodies, like snails, clams, mussels, octopuses, and squids (an invertebrate is an animal without a backbone). Most mollusks come equipped with a signature shell to lug around.

SPECIES: *Ba humbugi*

HABITAT: The island of Viti Levu in Fiji

TINY SNAILS: *Ba humbugi* isn't the only tiny snail on the block. There's actually a species of sea snail that's named for its minuscule size—the ittibittium. Ittibittium grow up to a quarter inch long, max!

SMOOTH-HEADED BLOBFISH

No hair here!

A very blobby body

What do you call a blobby fish with a smooth head? The smooth-headed blobfish, of course!

Psychrolutes marcidus is one of eleven known species swimming in the family Psychrolutidae, commonly known as blobfishes. The family's other common names don't get much more flattering—they are also called toadfishes or fathead **sculpins** (a sculpin is a type of fish from the order Scorpaeniformes known for living on the ocean floor).

While its appearance may be as unfortunate as its name, the blobfish's body is actually quite functional. Residing at the bottom of the ocean between 2,000 and 4,000 feet deep off the coast of

Australia and New Zealand, these blobs are constantly under a lot of pressure—water pressure, that is! Thanks to the low muscle mass and soft bones that make their body blobby, they are able to withstand the pressure and thrive.

Blobfishes pass their days hovering around like lazy blobs, waiting for unsuspecting sea creatures such as urchins, crabs, or mollusks to pass their way. They barely have to lift their heads to swallow up their prey.

SPECIES: *Psychrolutes marcidus*

HABITAT: The ocean floor off the coast of Australia and New Zealand

AND THE AWARD GOES TO . . . In 2013, the smooth-headed blobfish was named World's Ugliest Animal by the Ugly Animal Preservation Society!

BLUE-FOOTED BOOBY

Once known as "bobo" by Spanish explorers

Sports bright blue feet

A family of boobies

Back in the sixteenth century when Spanish explorers first ventured to the Galapagos Islands in the Pacific Ocean, they encountered many animals they had never seen before—including an unusual bird with a funny way of walking. Legend claims that the bird's silly, uncoordinated gait reminded the Spanish of clowns, so they called it *bobo*, which means "foolish" or "silly" in Spanish. "Bobo" later evolved to "booby" among English speakers.

As for the "blue-footed" in this bird's common name, well . . . just look at it!

Those eye-catching feet aren't just a fashion statement. The male blue-footed booby puts them to work. During his courtship dance, the male will stamp, swagger, and perform high-stepping moves while pointing his bill up in the air. The brighter blue the feet, the more attractive the male booby is to the females.

Although boobies are clumsy on land, they are incredible swimmers and flyers. While flying over

SPECIES: *Sula nebouxii*

HABITAT: While 70 percent of the world's population of blue-footed boobies live in the Galapagos Islands, they can be found all along the Pacific coast from Peru to Southern California.

YUM! Anchovies may be the least popular pizza topping, but they are a favorite meal for the dive-bombing booby!

29

the ocean, they use their binocular-like vision to spot schools of small fish swimming tightly together.

When they are ready for a snack, blue-footed boobies fold their wings back and dive headfirst from heights as lofty as 80 feet to capture their prey. To protect their heads from the impact, they have air sacs around their skull that cushion the blow.

They don't always have to take the dive, however: Blue-footed boobies have also been observed catching flying fish in midair!

2

MAGICAL NAMES

Nature can feel like a magical place when you wander—and wonder!—around in it. It's no surprise, then, that scientists sometimes reference fantasy or folklore when choosing animal names.

While the animals in this chapter might not have any "magical" powers, they are pretty wonder-inspiring. Don't believe in dragons? Wait until you meet the **FLYING DRAGONS** that soar through the jungles of Southeast Asia. What about unicorns? Our oceans are teeming with them! **UNICORNFISH**, that is. Love Greek mythology? Get ready to come face-to-face with the **HERCULES BEETLE**.

But be warned: There are also some fearsomely fantastical beasts lurking in this chapter, including "ghosts" and a "yeti." If you find yourself reading this chapter before bed, sleep tight and hope that the **GOBLIN SHARKS** don't bite!

Covered in pink armor plates

PINK FAIRY

The tiniest armadillo

I t might sound strange to describe anything with claws and armored plates as a "pink fairy," but the pink fairy armadillo earns its moniker. This "little armored one" (the direct translation of *armadillo* from Spanish) is the tiniest of all armadillos. Weighing in at less than half a pound and measuring only 3.5 to 4.5 inches long, it's easy to see

ARMADILLO

how this magical creature got named "fairy." As for the "pink," look no further than its twenty-four rosy-hued plates of armor.

Those stylish armor plates aren't just for looks, though. They also help protect the pink fairy armadillo. The last plate of armor is called the butt plate. Pink fairies spend most of their time underground, and they use the butt plate to pack soil behind them and cover the holes they call home, protecting their **burrows** from predators.

These fairies aren't finicky eaters; they eat whatever they can find underground, which means lots of ants and ant **larvae**, with a few other insects and worms thrown into the mix from time to time. But they are ferociously finicky when it comes to their habitat. They get extremely stressed if anything in their environment is unusual or out of place, making them difficult to observe in captivity. So, no, the pink fairy armadillo should not be kept as a pet, despite how cute it is!

SPECIES: *Chlamyphorus truncatus*

HABITAT: The sandy plains and dry grasslands of central Argentina

AND TO COMPLETE THE ENSEMBLE . . . The fashionable *pichiciego*, as it's known by the Argentineans, coordinates its fabulous pink armor with a silky coat of yellow-white fur that masks its face and fluffs its belly.

Named for a folkloric demon

GOBLIN SHARK

Belongs to the Mitsukurinidae shark family

If you're terrified of meeting a creature called a goblin shark, fear not—chances are slim that you will ever see one in the wild, because they live deep, deep down in the ocean where it is dark and creepy. If you ever *do* see one, though, get ready for a fright: With its ghostly coloration, unusual shape, and fearsome teeth, the goblin shark truly looks like a mythological monster.

In fact, the name "goblin shark" is rooted in folklore. This shark's weird, protruding nose reminded Japanese fishermen of a long-nosed, red-faced demon found in Japanese folklore called a *tengu*. They dubbed the shark *tengu-zame*, which translates to "goblin shark."

As if that's not spooky enough, you might say this species has come back from the dead. Not literally, of course, but as the only living member of Mitsukurinidae, a shark family that dates back to the time of the dinosaurs,

SPECIES: *Mitsukurina owstoni*

HABITAT: Coastal shelves around the world

SAY "AHH": Goblin sharks can open their mouths up to 111 degrees wide! If you could open your mouth 111 degrees, your bottom jaw would rest on your chest. We pitiful humans can only open our mouths 50 degrees.

the goblin shark is considered a **living fossil** (an animal that closely resembles extinct species and hasn't changed much over millions of years).

So, does that long, sword-like snout have a purpose beyond scaring the living daylights out of us? Scientists still aren't exactly sure. Their best guess is that the nose has super-sensitive electrical receptors to help the goblin shark locate prey. Considering where it lives—between 900 and 4,300 feet deep—the goblin shark can't be a picky eater, so it focuses its attention (and sword) in the direction of several kinds of **cephalopods**, **crustaceans** (animals belonging to the Crustacea subphylum, including shrimp and crabs), and fish.

How the goblin shark eats is the stuff of nightmares. It thrusts its mouth forward several inches to snatch unsuspecting prey, a process that scientists refer to as **slingshot feeding.** It would be like you throwing your mouth out 7 inches away from your face to take a bite! And it happens *fast—* the goblin shark can open and close its mouth quicker than a cobra strikes!

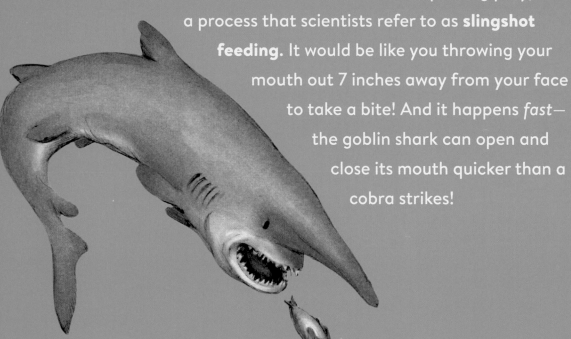

FLYING
Glides between jungle trees

DRAGON
Belongs to the Draco genus

Dragons aren't real. Or are they? Depends on what you mean by "dragon." If a flying lizard comes to mind, then you're in luck. All you have to do is journey to the jungles of Southeast Asia, where you can encounter some of the forty-two recognized species of lizards falling under the genus *Draco* (dragon), including *Draco volans*, commonly known as the flying dragon.

Sadly, flames are not a feature of *Draco volans*. However, as its common name suggests, flying is. Well, sort of . . .

The flying dragon does not actually fly; rather, it glides from tree to tree with the help of a group of elongated ribs that it can stretch out and shorten at will. Linking each rib is some loose

SPECIES: *Draco volans*

HABITAT: Tropical rain forests of Southeast Asia

GOOD LUCK, BABIES! Female flying dragons lay their eggs in holes they dig on the forest floor. They stand guard for about a day to protect their future fliers from predators and then scurry back up to the safety of the trees, letting nature take its course when it comes to their babies' survival—before they even hatch!

skin that, when the ribs are extended, acts as a wing, called a **patagium** (the plural is patagia). When the lizard sticks its forearms out to 90 degrees, its patagia reach full extension, turning the dragon into a glider and allowing it to "fly." After the dragon catches a gust of wind under its patagia, it uses its skinny tail to steer as it glides as far as 100 feet through the jungle air.

Terrified yet? No need to bring your sword or shield to confront this creature. Flying dragons are only about 9 inches long including their tail and spend almost all of their time up in the trees, living the life of an **insectivore**, feeding on ants and other tiny insects.

The trees offer much-needed protection, too. The jungle floor is a dangerous place for such a small animal, thanks to all the snakes and other lizards who would gladly slay these tiny dragons for a snack!

Look at those colorful patagia!

TINY DRAGONS

There are more dragons to meet! Many of the approximately 350 identified members of the Agamidae family of lizards have common names that include "dragon," including these four.

THORNY DRAGON *(Moloch horridus)* This
Australian lizard is also known as the thorny devil, and true to both names, its body is covered in tiny, thorn-like spikes that help protect it from predators. "Clever devil" might also be a fitting name, because this lizard has a crafty method for getting water in the dry desert: As dew condenses on the thorny dragon's body overnight, the moisture travels along little grooves in the lizard's scales until it reaches the mouth. Refreshing!

BEARDED DRAGON *(genus Pogona)* Ever wonder what human beards are used for? Warmth? Storing food for later? Braiding into little bows? Well, bearded dragons use their "beards"—which are actually rows of pointy scales along the throat—to communicate. By inflating its throat to different sizes and changing its color, the bearded dragon sends messages to its fellow dragons, like "Back off, I'm ready to tussle!"

EVERYWHERE!

BLOODSUCKERS

(genus Calotes) Don't worry, no vampires here—these bloodsuckers get their name from the bloodred head that males proudly display to impress females during the breeding season, not their dietary habits. The bloodsucker does have a pretty frightening style of eating, though: With teeth designed to grab, not tear, the bloodsucker takes hold of insects or rodents and swallows them whole!

PAINTED DRAGON

(Ctenophorus pictus) The painted dragon's body is covered in colors and patterns that help it blend in with its desert environment. But when it's time to woo, things sometimes get blue—bright blue! In order to attract female dragons, different parts of the male dragon's body change colors, turning flashy blue or shiny yellow-orange.

KOMODO DRAGON

Named for Komodo Island

Largest lizard in the world!

What creature has a large, powerful tail, a keen sense of smell, and sixty razor-sharp teeth it uses to scarf down up to 80 percent of its own body weight in prey in a single feeding? Your first thought might be a shark— but what if we told you that this creature roams on land?

The Komodo dragon, found only on a few Indonesian islands—including Komodo Island, the dragon's namesake—might just be the closest thing on Earth to a mythological dragon. Growing up to 10 feet long, it's much bigger than the flying lizards of the genus *Draco*—in fact, it's the largest lizard in the world!—and while it doesn't breathe fire, it does have an equally deadly power: venom.

When a Komodo dragon bites prey with its large, serrated teeth, the venom produced by glands in its mouth can put the prey into shock by lowering its blood pressure, slowing its heartbeat, and preventing its blood from clotting. This is one dangerous dragon!

SPECIES: *Varanus komodoensis*

HABITAT: *A few Indonesian islands, including Komodo Island*

SENSES SHAKE-UP: Like a snake, the Komodo dragon can smell with its tongue! After the dragon sticks its forked yellow tongue out to grab a sample of air, organs in its mouth analyze the air sample and detect the "scent" of potential prey.

Much like a shark, the Komodo dragon has a keen sense of smell and can detect injured prey from up to a mile away. But they're not always in a hurry to chase down their food. Komodo dragons are pretty slow and clumsy, so they tend to hide and lie in wait. When Timor deer, water buffalo, or wild pigs pass by, the Komodo lurches out and grabs a meal.

For such a powerful animal, Komodo dragons have a pretty difficult upbringing. They start off as an egg about the size of a grapefruit in a nest they must share with between fifteen and thirty dragon siblings. Once they hatch, they run as fast as they can to the nearest tree and scamper up it. Why? If they stay on the ground, they'll get snatched up by hungry adult dragons waiting nearby!

And the hardships don't end there. For the next four years, until they are big enough to hold their own against the adult dragons, young Komodos must find ways to survive up in the trees. This means eating as many tiny insects, geckos, and birds' eggs they can find until they are big enough to return to the ground and defend themselves against other Komodos.

A hatching Komodo dragon

44

LEAFY SEADRAGON

Has leaf-like strands hanging off its body

Dragon-shaped body

With its slender body, long tail, and back full of sharp spines, this strange sea creature resembles those ferocious fire-breathing lizards of myth. But not to fear—this little "dragon" isn't any more dangerous than the flying dragon lizard. The leafy seadragon only grows up to 14 inches long and it doesn't breathe fire. Heck, it doesn't even have teeth!

Fortunately, it doesn't need teeth to eat. The seadragon slurps thousands of microscopic, shrimp-like animals for its meals. Even stranger, leafies don't have stomachs to store their food, so they must constantly search the sea for food in order to stay alive.

Not only is this seadragon not a real dragon, its "leaves" aren't even real leaves—although they certainly look like it! They are actually threads of skin hanging from the seadragon's head, body, and tail. These "leaves" serve as camouflage, helping seadragons blend in with kelp and seagrass.

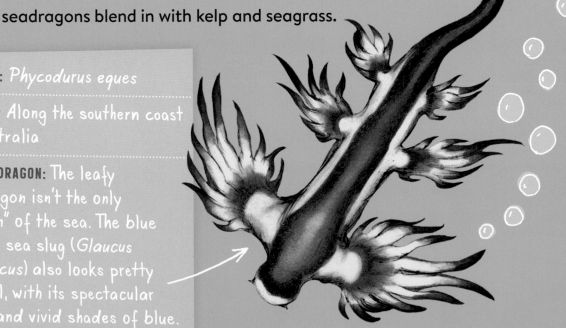

SPECIES: *Phycodurus eques*

HABITAT: Along the southern coast of Australia

POISON DRAGON: The leafy seadragon isn't the only "dragon" of the sea. The blue dragon sea slug (*Glaucus atlanticus*) also looks pretty magical, with its spectacular shape and vivid shades of blue.

Fortunately, the seadragon's unusual design is well suited for all that free roaming. While the seadragon's relative, the seahorse, has a gripping tail that it uses to anchor itself to a single spot, the seadragon's leafy tail helps it float freely through the sea in search of grub.

The leafy sea dragon has no known predators, in part because so many of its characteristics keep predators away: Its highly developed camouflage makes it an underwater hide-and-seek champion, the spines on its back are sharp, and it has very little meat on its body.

When it comes to the care and protection of their babies, members of the family Syngnathidae leave it to the dads. The male leafy seadragon carries up to 250 bright pink eggs in a special **brood pouch** under his tail until the eggs hatch.

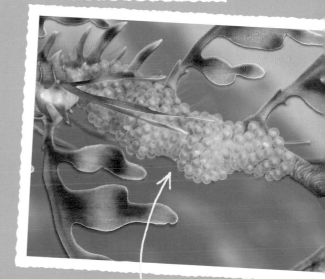

Eggs on a male seadragon's tail

AUSTRALIAN GHOST SHARK

Looks like a phantom of the deep sea

The Australian ghost shark—quick, three guesses where it can be found!—has shiny, silvery skin sprinkled with black dots, giving it a specter-like appearance as it haunts the murky depths.

To make matters even spookier, this shark is a member of the "living dead." No, it's not a zombie, but like the goblin shark, the Australian ghost shark is what scientists call a **living fossil**, because it hasn't changed much over millions of years.

The other curious feature of this ghostly shark? That dangling snout! It's no wonder this creature has inspired nicknames like the elephant shark and the plough-nose chimera. In Greek mythology, a chimera is a part-lion, part-snake, part-goat hybrid. Like the chimera, *Callorhinchus milii* looks like a bit of a mash-up—a shark mixed with an elephant mixed with a mythical monster!

So what is that nose good for? Fish in the family Callorhinchidae, including the Australian ghost shark, spook their prey by using their long, flexible snouts to dig around the seafloor and root out small fish and **invertebrates** for food.

While the Australian ghost shark doesn't have a ferocious bite, the venomous stinger on its **dorsal fin** provides plenty of fright!

Chimera

SPECIES: *Callorhinchus milii*

HABITAT: The waters south of Australia and New Zealand

TALK ABOUT A REAL GHOST!
To date, only a single specimen of the Bahamas ghost shark (*Chimaera bahamaensis*), another specter of the deep, has been seen.

49

HERCULES BEETLE

One of the world's strongest beetles

50

n Greek mythology, Hercules was the strongest man on earth, so it's fitting that the hercules beetle is believed to be one of the strongest beetles on earth.

You may already know that itty-bitty ants can heft up to 50 times their own weight. Well, the mighty hercules beetle can reportedly throw around objects 850 times its weight! That's like an adult human lifting nine elephants!

This beetle's other notable feature is the huge horn on the head of the males. You might be quick to think that the hercules beetle uses his horn in battle, but you would only be half right. While beetles sometimes use their horns to fight one another for the right to feed and breed, those horns also come in handy when they need to escape predators. When threatened by foes mightier than they can handle, hercules beetles use their horns to dig into soft soil or leaf litter so they can hide until the enemies pass.

If that horn reminds you of a much larger animal, you might be interested to know that this little hercules belongs to a group of beetles commonly called rhinoceros beetles.

SPECIES: *Dynastes hercules*

HABITAT: Tropical rain forests of Central and South America

PUPA POOP: Moths may make their cocoons out of silk, but they've got nothing on hercules beetles. These mighty insects use their own poop to make their pupa chambers! (The pupa chamber is where the larvae hang out before they mature into adult beetles. At this stage of development, the insect is called a **pupa**.)

MOONRAT

No, the moonrat does not live on the moon—and it's not even a rat! So how did it get stuck with this name?

Let's break it into two parts. The "moon" part comes from the bright-white fur that moonrats often sport and the fact that they are **nocturnal** (an animal that spends its nights awake and its days catching ZZZs). As far as the "rat" part, well . . . that's an honest mistake. While the moonrat is definitely not a rat, it would probably win top prize at a rat look-alike contest.

So if it's not a rat, what is it? Rather than being a part of the order Rodentia, like rats, the moonrat orbits in the order Eulipotyphla.

Eulipotyphla translates to "truly fat and blind" and includes other earth-based dwellers like shrews, hedgehogs, and moles.

What does the moonrat do at night while the world is sleeping? It feasts! Moonrats eat pretty much whatever they can find, from forest fruit to earthworms to **arthropods** (animals like spiders and shrimp that have a protective **exoskeleton** covering their outside instead of a skeleton on their inside).

Some moonrats have areas of darker fur.

52

You would probably rather be sent to the moon than visit a moonrat's home. They mark their area by spewing a powerful spray from their anal glands. The scent has been described as falling somewhere between ammonia and garlic gone bad. When a moonrat is near, plug your nose and be prepared to blast off!

SPECIES: *Echinosorex gymnura*

HABITAT: The mangrove and swamp forests of Myanmar, Thailand, and Borneo

BUT IT LOOKS LIKE A PANDA . . . The moonrat is far from the only animal whose common name is a total misnomer. The killer whale is a dolphin, not a whale, and the red panda is closer to a weasel than a panda!

UNICORN-FISH

No one has ever found a four-legged unicorn, but did you know that there are "unicorns" that live in the ocean? The fish of the genus *Naso* are commonly called unicornfish thanks to the horn or **rostral protuberance** (as scientists call it) sticking out of the forehead of several species in the genus. And the common names for *Naso* species are even better—there's the bulbnose unicornfish, the humpback unicornfish, the elegant unicornfish, and the horseface unicornfish, to name just a few!

While you might think that their horns would make them easy to spot, unicornfish have a magic trick up their sleeve to help them avoid detection:

54

When frightened, they can quickly change colors depending on their mood and environment and "disappear." If you *do* manage to spot a unicornfish, you will probably find it swimming around reefs, feeding on algae and plankton . . . or something grosser. The rostral protuberance of some unicornfish grows longer as the fish ages and can get in the way when the unicornfish tries to feed on algae along the seabed. So as its horn gets longer, the fish must change its food source, and some unicornfish find themselves eating the poop of other fish!

GENUS: *Naso*

HABITAT: Indo–Pacific Ocean

THAT OTHER UNICORNFISH: The *Eumecicthys fiski* unicornfish is an entirely different species. Far less is known about this super rare unicorn of the sea, but we do know this much: With a spike protruding out between its big, bulging eyes and a jaw full of pointy teeth, it's more likely to appear in your nightmares than your fantasies!

55

WACKY SCIENTIFIC NAME ALERT!

Not a magician but pretty magical-looking!

AGRA CADABRA

The *Agra* genus is a group of beetles with more than five hundred identified and fully described species—and more than a thousand others that have yet to be fully described and assigned a specific name.

When it comes to naming *Agra* beetles, scientist Terry Erwin is the undisputed master— he's named hundreds of *Agra* species, and he's having fun with it! In addition to the magical-sounding *Agra cadabra*, he has named beetles in this genus after celebrities like Arnold Schwarzenegger (*Agra schwarzeneggeri*) and Kate Winslet (*Agra katewinsletae*), fictional characters like Yoda (*Agra yoda*) and Ichabod Crane (*Agra ichabod*), mythical creatures like the yeti (*Agra yeti*) and Sasquatch (*Agra sasquatch*), and even the feeling you might have if you found your home overrun with beetles—*Agra vation*!

The *Agra* beetles are commonly referred to as elegant canopy beetles, thanks to their slender build and the fact that they live in jungle canopies. Their wide feet come with pads that help them grip plants and leaves, where they can often be found hanging upside down, resting and hiding from predators.

Agra katewinsletae

SPECIES: *Agra cadabra*

HABITAT: Jungles of Central and South America

SMELL YOU LATER! When threatened, *Agra* beetles aggravate predators by releasing a special, stinky secretion.

Very hairy arms!

YETI CRAB

SPECIES: *Kiwa hirsuta*

HABITAT: Hydrothermal vents on the ocean floor

HYDRO-WHAT? A hydrothermal vent is an opening in the seafloor through which hot water from below the earth's crust flows out.

This hairy critter, first found clinging to **hydrothermal vents** along the Pacific-Antarctic Ridge during a 2005 expedition led by scientist Bob Vrijenhoek, boasts two epic names: Its genus name, *Kiwa*, is a reference to the Polynesian goddess of **crustaceans**, while its common name, yeti crab, is a nod to the legendary (and very hairy) yeti, rumored to live in the frozen and remote regions of the Himalayas.

Why a yeti? Just look at those hairy arms! All that hair reminded Vrijenhoek and his team of scientists of the fabled yeti, also known as the Abominable Snowman.

The feathery, hair-like spines (called **setae**) found on the yeti crab aren't just for show; they are fully functional, helping the yeti crab grow its own food. That's right: The yeti crab's main source of food is the **bacteria** (a kind of single-cell microorganism) that grows in its own hair! Sounds pretty gross, but let's not judge nature.

Rather than living in extremely cold climates tens of thousands of feet above sea level like its monstrous namesake, the yeti crab lives 8,500 feet below the surface of the sea in spots where extremely hot water (700°F) meets freezing Antarctic waters. Scientists call these rare spots **Goldilocks Zones**. The term refers to a tiny area (only about 1 square yard) where cold water collides with the heat spewing from hydrothermal vents, creating a climate that is not too hot, not too cold, but just right. More than seven hundred yeti crabs have been observed cramming into a single Goldilocks Zone, where they spend their entire lives.

WONDERPUS

The octopus genus *Wunderpus* gets its name from the German word for "wonder," *wünder*. And it's no wonder—just look at it!

Usually, the wonderpus appears copper-brown, with spots and stripes of white sprinkled across its head and arms. However, while the spots and stripes on the wonderpus always retain their shapes, these creatures can change color in the blink of an eye! How? Like all octopuses, the wonderpus is able to control the hue and contrast of the **chromatophores** in its skin.

Chromatophores are one of the most amazing structures in nature and are found in all kinds of animals, from fish to amphibians. These special cells house tiny pouches of color pigments like black, orange, red, yellow, and brown. When the pouches are squeezed, the color appears at the top of the pouches and the creature seems to change color. The wonderpus's

thousands of chromatophores are controlled by special dedicated nerves and muscles. It's like a superpower!

The wonderpus can also change its texture, so it can look like rocks, coral, or other objects it encounters in the ocean. Blending in protects wonderpuses from predators and makes them a favorite sight for divers. Their camouflage skills also help them sneak up on small fish, shellfish, and **crustaceans** and scoop them into their tiny beaked mouths.

Need help telling two wonderpuses apart? Look at the white spot pattern on their Y-shaped heads. No two wonderpuses have the exact same pattern.

SPECIES: *Wunderpus photogenicus*

HABITAT: The shallow waters surrounding Vanuatu, Papua New Guinea, Indonesia, Malaysia, and the Philippines

SPEAKING OF CURIOUSLY NAMED OCTOPUSES . . .
Another eight-limbed sea dweller is called the dumbo octopus—and no offense, but you would have to be a bit of a dumbo yourself to not see why! With its big, floppy ears, the dumbo octopus looks more than a little like the famous Disney pachyderm.

Dumbo octopus

3

FIERCE NAMES

AHH!

EEK!!

This chapter is not for the faint of heart! You are about to meet some of the most ferocious-sounding animals on earth, from the **VAMPIRE SQUID** to the **HICKORY HORNED DEVIL**. Were scientists just trying to scare us when they came up with these fearsome names? While some of these critters are all bark and no bite—we're looking at you, **LIONHEAD RABBIT**—most of them earn their monikers with fierce appearances and even fiercer behaviors. Just wait until you see how the **SPINED ASSASSIN BUG** kills its prey!

Often, the way these animals look and behave are adaptations that allow them to survive and thrive in unlikely places. In addition to meeting surface critters with fear-inspiring names, we'll explore some of the terrors lurking deep down in the sea. With cold temperatures and enough pressure to crush a car, it takes a pretty fierce—and fiercely named!—critter to call the deepest depths of the oceans home.

HELLBENDER

Looks like it came from someplace terrifying!

So slimy!

Next time you are swimming in a country stream, would you rather come face to face with a hellbender or a snot otter? It wouldn't make a lick of difference, because they are the same animal!

Legend holds that the hellbender got its name from early European settlers in the United States. After laying eyes on the freakish creature, they thought it looked like it had crawled out of the depths of hell.

As if hellbender isn't bad enough, these slimy salamanders are sometimes called snot otters (even though they are definitely *not* otters!) thanks to the slimy mucus they secrete all over their bodies when threatened. Other head-scratching nicknames include lasagna lizards and devil dogs.

Growing from 12 to 29 inches long and weighing up to 5 pounds, the hellbender is not only ugly, but also rather large for a salamander. In fact, the eastern hellbender is the largest known salamander in the Americas.

Being amphibians, hellbenders can move around outside of water, but because their skin absorbs the oxygen they need from fast-moving water, they tend to find a safe spot in a good location (like under a big rock in a swift stream) and stay put.

They spend most of their time waiting for an unsuspecting meal to swim by. Because they are **nocturnal** feeders, they rely on touch and smell to find prey—often crayfish, which can make up 90 percent of the hellbender's diet!

SPECIES: *Cryptobranchus alleganiensis*

HABITAT: Eastern and central United States

WHAT AN HONOR! Move over, state birds! In 2019, the hellbender was named the official amphibian of the state of Pennsylvania.

SPINED ASSASSIN BUG

Body covered in prickly spines

A super stealthy killer

Gardens can be a dangerous place for little bugs—especially when spined assassins perch among the flowers, just waiting for their next meal!

The spined assassin bug, as its name suggests, is a straight-up assassin. It moves stealthily among plants and flowers, blending in thanks to all those spines covering its body. When an unsuspecting caterpillar, ladybug, or roach stumbles by, the assassin pounces with a flash kick of its spiny front legs and attacks the poor critter that made the mistake of crossing this killer's path.

The spined assassin's method of eating is truly something to behold: It stabs its prey repeatedly with its strong, fang-like beak until it reaches deep enough within its victim to inject a special mix of digestive enzymes. That's right, the assassin's beak

doubles as an injection device, and once it releases its enzymes, what were once the functioning innards of a living creature turn into some truly nutritious goo! With little more than a *whurp* the spined assassin slurps it up.

Despite their downright disturbing way of staying fed, spined assassins are friends of gardeners because they slay many common garden pests.

67

SPECIES: *Sinea diadema*

HABITAT: The southern United States and northern Mexico

NO KISS FOR ME, THANKS! *A close cousin of the assassin bug is the "kissing bug." Sounds sweet, but think twice before you pucker up! Kissing bugs have been known to suck human blood. And since they can carry Chagas disease, which is potentially fatal, they could be considered assassins as well!*

LIONHEAD RABBIT

Boasts a fluffy mane of hair

SPECIES: *Oryctolagus cuniculus*

HABITAT: First bred in Belgium but now raised as a pet in many countries

WHAT DELICATE EARS! While it might have an overgrown mane, the lionhead's 2- to 3-inch-long ears are rather small compared to those of other rabbits.

Neither the temperament nor the size of this rabbit warrants such a ferocious name, but just look at that lovely mane! With a huge poof of hair hanging around its head, it's easy to see how this hopper earned the common name lionhead.

King of the jungle!

Believed to be a mix between a Netherland dwarf rabbit and a Swiss fox rabbit, the lionhead can be found in homes all over the world. That's because, unlike real lions, these little beasts can be tamed and make great pets! They can even be trained to follow commands like "come" and "play."

There are two types of lionhead rabbits: single-maned and double-maned. The "single" or "double" refers to the number of copies of the **gene** for the mane the rabbit has. (Genes carry information from parents to their offspring and determine which characteristics the offspring will inherit.)

If the lionhead has a single copy of the mane gene, much of the extra fluff it has as a young bunny will shed by the time it becomes an adult rabbit, leaving only a mane around its head and sometimes spots on its chest and bottom. Those with two copies of the gene, however, retain more of their fluff as they grow older, and also develop what appears to be a skirt of fur around their hindquarters.

HAGFISH

More like "slimefish!"

FAMILY: Myxinidae

HABITAT: The ocean floor

HAPPY HAGFISH DAY! Hagfish Day is celebrated every year on the third Wednesday of October. It's designed to raise awareness about the need to protect all species, even the not-so-cute ones.

If there was an award for the most disgusting animal on earth, the hagfish would probably win in a landslide.

Hagfish are shaped like eels, but with no eyes and a jawless mouth. Instead of teeth, they have two rows of tooth-like formations made of keratin (the same material that makes up your fingernails).

The hagfish is the animal kingdom's slime champion—it has been reported that a single hagfish can produce 5 gallons of slime in just a few minutes! Even more amazing, when a hagfish's slime makes contact with water, it can expand to almost 10,000 times its original size. The threads that make up the slime are incredibly strong—so strong, in fact, that researchers are studying how we might use hagfish slime instead of nylon to make certain kinds of clothing.

That super-strong slime comes in handy for the hagfish, too. Remarkably, the hagfish has the ability to "sneeze" out any slime that gets in its nostrils—and this helps them fend off foes. In fact, the hagfish produces enough slime to suffocate its would-be predators!

If you're thinking the hagfish couldn't get any grosser, think again. When they eat, hagfish lunge face-first into the carcasses of animals as large as sharks and whales. They use their mouths to drill into the carcasses, twisting and turning their bodies to go deeper.

It might sound horrific, but it's actually a good thing—hagfish play an important role in the ocean ecosystem by cleaning up dead animals. Without hagfish, a lot of waste would build up, making the water nasty to swim in. Thank you, hagfish!

POISON DART

Arrow or dart? Pick your poison. All of the frog species in the family Dendrobatidae are commonly referred to as either poison dart frogs or poison arrow frogs.

Despite their tiny size—adults range between 0.59 inches and 2.4 inches in length, and weigh a mere 1 ounce on average—poison dart frogs are considered one of the most toxic animals on earth.

While not all poison dart frogs have the same level of toxicity, some species can kill with a single touch!

FAMILY: Dendrobatidae

HABITAT: Central and South America

POISON POWER: The golden poison dart frog is tiny enough to sit in a teaspoon, yet packs poison potent enough to kill up to twenty thousand mice!

FROG

Golden poison frogs

In fact, people once used the poison these frogs secrete as a "secret weapon" to tip their darts and arrows while hunting, hence those common names.

Where does all that poison come from? A popular theory claims that poison dart frogs get their poison from their prey. In the process of eating one animal, such as a beetle or termite or ant, the frog absorbs the chemicals it needs to continue producing poison.

Several species of poison dart frogs are **aposematic**, which means that their striking coloration serves as a warning to jungle predators who might be hankering for a frogs' legs lunch. The bright colors signal "poisonous!" Other less toxic species of poison dart frogs use their less flashy coloration to elevate their **crypsis** game, making them highly proficient in blending in with their natural surroundings.

The specific common names of poison dart frogs are as entertaining as their family name. There's the phantasmal poison frog (genus *Epipedobates*), the thumbnail poison frog (genus *Ranitomeya*), and the rocket frog (genus *Colostethus*), among others.

BONE-EATING

SNOT FLOWER WORM

Looks like a flower covered in mucus

This gruesome worm's common name is a direct translation of its scientific name (*Osedax* = bone-eating; *mucofloris* = snot flower), and everything you need to know about this unusual creature is right there in its name.

This sea-dwelling worm "eats" the bones of dead animals—specifically, any bone that sinks to the ocean floor. While they typically dine on the bones of whales, they have also been found rooted to steak bones that have been thrown into the ocean by humans. Their bone-eating ways have earned them another fun nickname: "zombie worms."

The "eating" part of this worm's common name isn't exactly correct, though. Bone-eating snot flower worms don't have mouths or a digestive system—and that means

SPECIES: *Osedax mucofloris*

HABITAT: The North Atlantic

SNOT FLOWER'S RELATIVES: Other species of bone-eating worms include *Osedax antarcticus* and *Osedax japonicus*, which were both named after the place where they were first discovered (can you guess where?), *Osedax roseus*, which is named for its red color, and *Osedax frankpressi*, named to honor scientist Frank Press.

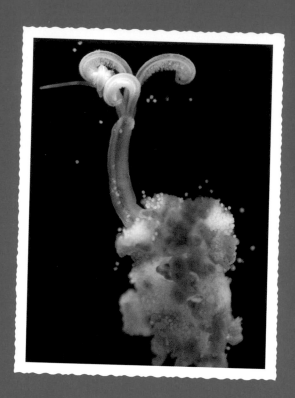

they don't have a gut or a butt, either! To "eat," they secrete an acid that breaks down the bone so they can absorb nutrients from it.

Now you see why it's called "bone-eating," but what about the "snot flower" bit? It has to do with how these worms absorb those nutrients. In order to access the fat inside the bones where nutrients can be found, the worm drills its root-like structures down into the bone, connecting itself to the bone like a flower planted in the earth.

The worm's resemblance to a flower doesn't stop there. Several of this creature's snotty-looking organs are outside its body instead of inside, giving it the appearance of a blooming flower covered in mucus.

Males and females are not created equal in the world of bone-eating snot flower worms. What you see rooted into a bone and "blossoming" are all female worms. To find a male worm, you have to look inside a female worm, where you can find up to 100 tiny male worms! When there is a big difference between the male and the female specimens of a single species—for example, the vastly different sizes of male and female bone-eating snot flower worms—it's called **sexual dimorphism**.

VAMPIRE

Has a vampire-like "cape"

SQUID

Not a real squid, but looks like one

The full translation of this sea beast's scientific name, *Vampyroteuthis infernalis*, is "vampire squid from hell." While not quite the depths of hell, this **nocturnal** squid does prowl around 5,000 to 8,000 feet below the surface of the ocean, making it one of the deepest-living ocean animals we know about.

Strictly speaking, the vampire squid is as much a vampire as it is a squid—which is to say, it's neither! If you're looking for two sharp fangs or a habit of bloodsucking, you won't find it here. This "vampire" gets its common name thanks to its bloodred coloration and the dark, cape-like shape it takes when it billows out the webbing connecting its eight arms.

A vampire squid takes a defensive position and illuminates a photophore.

And unlike vampires of legend, this squid is a passive eater, mostly feeding on something called **marine snow**—it might sound pretty, but it actually refers to bits of dead animals and the poop and snot of other sea creatures. As this "snow" floats down to the deep ocean depths, vampire squids gobble it up. Yum!

So why isn't it technically a squid? Vampire "squids" are the only known members of the order Vampyromorphida, making them distinct from octopuses and squids—although they share features with both. While squids have eight arms and two tentacles, these vampires only have eight arms, making them look more like an octopus. However, their arms more closely resemble the tentacles of a squid.

SPECIES: *Vampyroteuthis infernalis*

HABITAT: The deep sea

LIGHT SHOW: Vampire squids are **bioluminescent**, which means they can produce their own light. When faced with a potential predator, they activate **photophores** (bioluminescent organs) all over their body, creating a flashing light show that confuses and distracts their foe.

What's the difference between an arm and a tentacle when it comes to sea creatures? Arms tend to have tiny suckers lining their entire length, whereas tentacles usually have only a few suckers at the tips.

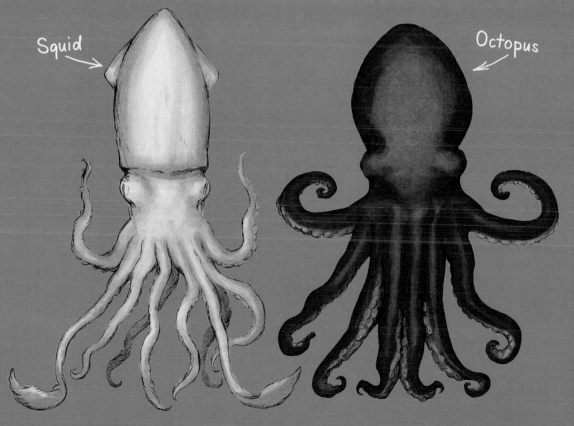

Squid

Octopus

HICKORY HORNED DEVIL

Feeds on hickory trees

Has spiky horns on its head

80

f a hickory is a kind of tree and a devil is a monster with horns, what on earth (or in hell) is a hickory horned devil? If you guessed a caterpillar that can grow as large as a hot dog—you're right!

These strange caterpillars might look like ferocious little devils, with several spiky orange horns sticking out of their heads, but that's just for shock and show. Thanks to their dangerous look, predators that typically pick on caterpillars, like chickens, tend to leave these harmless little devils alone.

To grow as big as they do, hickory horned devils eat the leaves of ash, walnut, pecan, and other hickory-type trees.

Then, after five weeks as a caterpillar, they find some soil to burrow down in for their next stage of life: the **pupa** stage. They go on to live for another one or two years as a pupa before hatching as an adult moth (known as the Regal or Royal Walnut moth).

As a moth, they will enjoy no food (they don't even have a moth mouth!) but will soar with a wingspan of up to 6 inches. Because they have only about a week to live as a moth, they spend that time mating and laying eggs for the next generation of hickory horned devils.

Regal moth

SPECIES: *Citheronia regalis*

HABITAT: The forests of the eastern and southern United States

THE ULTIMATE DISGUISE: The hickory horned devil often curls itself into a J shape. The shape, along with the caterpillar's colorization, makes it look like bird poop, which keeps it safe. Few predators are interested in adding bird poop to their menu!

81

ARROWTOOTH LIZARDFISH

Covered in lizard-like scales

Like other members of the family Synodontidae commonly known as lizardfish, the arrowtooth's slender, arrow-shaped body is covered in lizard-like scales and it has a mouth full of fearsome chompers.

But don't worry—it's totally safe to go in the water. These fish might sound terrifying, but they are less than a foot long and spend most of their time hiding in ocean sand with only their eyes sticking out, waiting to snag tiny fish that wander by. Humans aren't on the menu!

The arrowtooth lizardfish's scientific name is as fitting as its common name. *Synodus* is a combination of the

Look at all those teeth!

82

Greek words *syn* ("grown together") and *odus* ("teeth"), while *doaki* is a Latin-sounding version of the last name Doak, a reference to naturalist Wade Doak, who discovered the arrowtooth lizardfish while diving around the Poor Knights Islands off the coast of New Zealand.

SPECIES: *Synodus doaki*

HABITAT: The shallow waters surrounding Australia, Japan, East Africa, and Hawaii

SHARP TONGUE: In addition to their regular chompers, arrowtooth lizardfishes have spiny, sharp teeth covering their tongues.

DREADFUL

As if the arrowtooth lizardfish isn't fierce-sounding enough, here are four more creatures from the deep with names that will keep you awake at night!

FANGTOOTH FISH (family Anoplogastridae)

Any creature with large, dagger-like fangs is terrifying. It's a good thing the fangtooth fish is only 6 inches long! But smaller fish beware: The fangtooth has the largest teeth relative to its body of any animal in the world. With such an impressive set of teeth, you might think the fangtooth always swims around with its mouth open. But nope! Its huge fangs fit into special pockets in its skull when its mouth is closed.

BLACK SWALLOWER (Chiasmodon niger)

Thanks to the ginormous stomach hanging underneath it like a huge shopping bag, the black swallower can swallow fish bigger than itself—much bigger! In fact, they've been known to eat mackerels three times longer than themselves. Holy mackerel!

NAMES OF THE DEEP

VIPERFISH (genus *Chauliodus*)

With fearsome fangs that would
look more at home in the pit of a viper's mouth
than a fish's, this creature's name is pretty self-explanatory.
Naturally, other fish are frightened by the viperfish, so these
fanged fish must be clever and "go fishing" for their food by using
a tiny organ dangling off their bodies as a lure to attract prey.
What makes the viperfish's lure so, well, *alluring* is that it's
actually a **photophore** (a light-producing organ
found in many marine animals).

UMBRELLAMOUTH GULPER EEL

(*Eurypharynx pelecanoides*) This bad boy's
mouth is literally bigger than its body,
and opens wide like an umbrella to
gulp down prey larger than the eel itself!
It's also known as the pelican eel because
its hinged lower jaw resembles a pelican's. Like many deep-sea
animals, the gulper uses a photophore to attract prey. However,
while other creatures have this organ near the mouth, the
umbrellamouth gulper eel's photophore is found in its tail.

SCREAMING HAIRY ARMADILLO

Shrieks to scare predators

Covered in bristly hair

If you ever find yourself hiking in the Monte Desert in Argentina and you happen to see a small, hairy creature that starts screaming the second it sees you, you are probably staring at a *Chaetophractus vellerosus*, or screaming hairy armadillo.

The screaming hairy armadillo is covered in scales called **scutes** like other armadillos but is distinguished by the bristly hair on its armor, making it the hairiest of all armadillos. It also has the honor of being the tiniest of the hairy armadillos (though it is still more sizable than the teensy pink fairy armadillo—see page 32). From the tip of its nose to the tip of its tail, it measures between 12 and 22 inches long and weighs in at around 2 pounds.

What screaming hairy armadillos lack in size they make up for in screams. They rely on their shrill cry to scare away predators,

including human hunters and hunting dogs. Like other armadillos, they also use their burrowing abilities to protect themselves.

When not hiding from or screaming at potential predators, the screaming hairy armadillo is digging around for its own food. While they are not above foraging through the bodies of dead animals to find an insect or other **invertebrates** to eat, they mostly scavenge by digging in the sand. In fact, scientists have discovered that some of these screamers have stomach contents of more than 50 percent sand!

SPECIES: *Chaetophractus vellerosus*

HABITAT: Central and southern South America

HAIRY HYDRATION: You might think all that screaming would build up a thirst, but the screaming hairy armadillo's kidneys are highly efficient so it rarely needs to drink water.

TWICE-STABBED STINK BUG

The two red dots on its back look like wounds

Releases a nasty-smelling spray

Have you ever thought about changing your name? You certainly wouldn't be the only one. Some people legally change their names, and many actors and musicians adopt "stage names," like Bruno Mars and Lady Gaga.

Sometimes animals go through name changes, too—although it has less to do with what the animal wants to be called and more to do with scientists changing their minds! For instance, take *Cosmopepla lintneriana*, or the twice-stabbed stink bug as it is commonly known.

Danish zoologist Johann Christian Fabricius took the first stab at giving this stink bug a scientific name in 1798, dubbing it *Cimex carnifex*, but the name didn't stick. In 1865, scientists offered other names, including *Pentatoma bimaculata* and *Cosmopepla bimaculata*. Finally, in 1909, English **entomologist** G. W. Kirkaldy came along and gave a final—and successful—stab at naming the many-named stink bug. Kirkaldy dubbed it *Cosmopepla lintneriana* in honor of former New York State Entomologist Joseph Albert Lintner.

If your head is spinning with scientific names, it's probably easiest to remember this stinker's common name. The reason for the "stink" will be evident if you get too close to one. When you think of an animal that sprays some real sweet nasty

SPECIES: *Cosmopepla lintneriana*

HABITAT: North America

WHAT'S FOR DINNER? Stink bugs feed on an incredible variety of plants, from asparagus to peach trees, milk thistle, and even oats. They use their beak-like mouths to inject digestive enzymes into the plant and then suck up the digested goodies.

Stink bugs aren't picky when it comes to eating plants.

out of its behind, a skunk likely comes to mind. But the entire Pentatomidae family of bugs, commonly called stink bugs, do the same thing. Stink bugs even have ninja-like control over their two stink glands; they can spray from one gland or both, making sure to meet the threat level with the appropriate stink level.

As for the "twice-stabbed," look no further than the two red marks on top of the bug's black back. It looks like it was just stabbed in the back twice by a disloyal friend! This **aposematic** coloration warns predators to stay away by suggesting that this creature might be poisonous.

And indeed, whenever the twice-stabbed stink bug is irritated, it lets out a stinky liquid made of droplets that are partially poisonous. Now, that's an effective repellent!

4

MMMMM!!

DELICIOUS NAMES

YUMMY!

What were scientists thinking when they named the **BANANA SLUG** and the **PINEAPPLE FISH**? Maybe they were hungry for a fruit salad! It must have been breakfast time when they named the **PANCAKE TORTOISE**, and let's not forget dessert—there's the **HONEY BADGER**, the **CANDY-STRIPED HERMIT CRAB**, and the *GELAE BAEN* beetle. Looks like scientists have more on their minds than just the animals they study!

But you can't really blame them once you meet these critters. Most of them look a lot like the food they were named for. If you ever spot a **FRIED EGG JELLYFISH**, you might think someone just cracked an enormous egg into the ocean!

In this chapter, you're going to discover some new names, explore some exciting places, and quite possibly get very, very hungry. So bon appétit . . . er, delicious reading!

FRIED EGG

Don't eat! It only LOOKS like a tasty fried egg! →

JELLYFISH

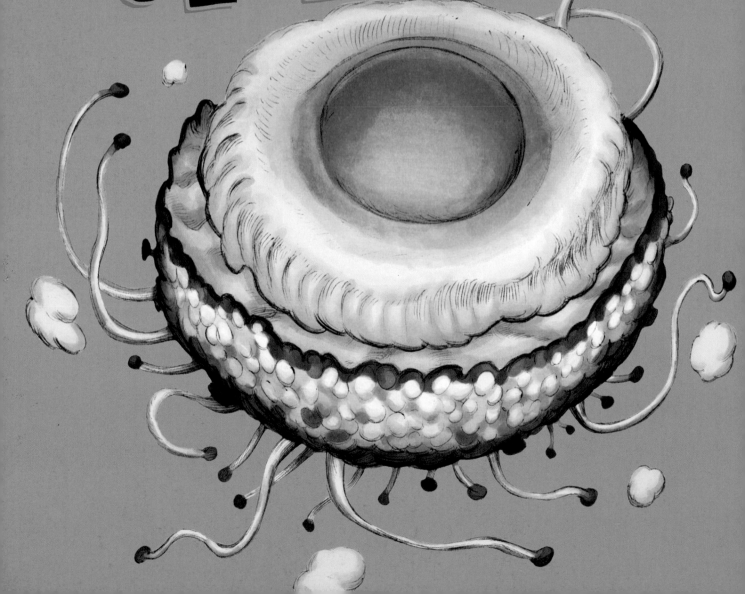

How do you like your eggs? Scrambled? Fried? Over easy with jelly?

While the **bell** (the dome-shaped top) of *Cotylorhiza tuberculata* definitely resembles an egg served sunny-side up, you probably wouldn't want to see those dangling purple bits on your breakfast plate! Not to fear, though—this jelly's stingers aren't harmful to humans.

Those stingers *can* spell trouble for the jelly's fellow sea creatures . . . but for others, they offer some much-needed protection. Certain fish, like mackerels, like to hang out close to the fried egg jellyfish and hitch a ride around the sea with it, relying on its stingers to protect them from their predators. Fried egg express!

You would think a name like the fried egg jellyfish would really set you apart. Well, think again: There are actually two species with the same common name! In addition to *Cotylorhiza tuberculata*, a larger jelly species—*Phacellophora camtschatica*—is also called the fried egg jellyfish. We can't blame whoever named them, though—they both look a lot like fried eggs!

SPECIES: *Cotylorhiza tuberculata*

HABITAT: The Mediterranean, Adriatic, and Aegean seas

THAT'S A BIG FRIED EGG! The average fried egg jellyfish is 14 inches in diameter.

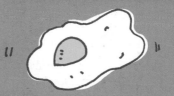

CANDY-STRIPED HERMIT CRAB

Has red and white striped legs like a candy cane

Like other hermit crabs, it finds a shell to live in

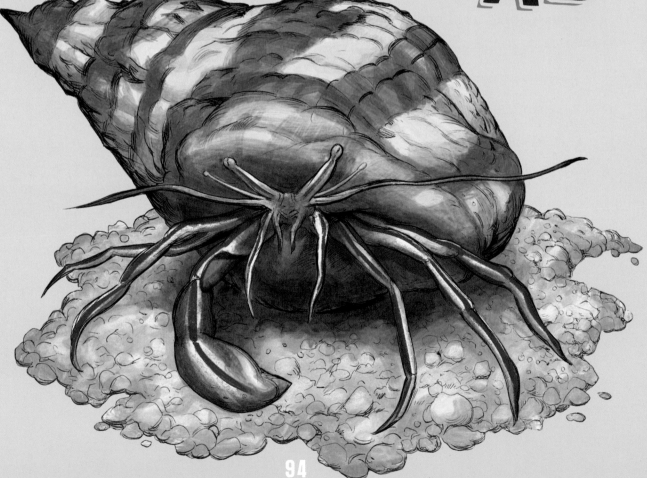

94

What's the coolest gift you've ever been given? For Molly Muller, it was probably when her grandmother, naturalist photographer Ellen Muller, named a species after her.

Ms. Muller accidentally discovered this less-than-an-inch-long crab while photographing a flaming reef lobster off the coast of Bonaire, a Dutch island near Venezuela. She named the species *mollymullerae* to "inspire [Molly] to continue the tradition of protecting the amazing and fragile diversity of marine life in Bonaire."

Pretty sweet, huh? Not nearly as sweet as the common name *Pylopaguropsis mollymullerae* got when Ms. Muller sent pictures of it to the Smithsonian Institution's National Museum of Natural History. After confirming it as a new species, Dr. Rafael Lemaitre, in consultation with Ms. Muller, conferred the common name "candy-striped hermit crab" upon the crab because its legs reminded them of candy canes. Can you blame them? Just look at those red and white stripes!

Candy cane legs aren't the only thing

Ellen Muller took several pictures of her discovery

SPECIES: *Pylopaguropsis mollymullerae*

HABITAT: The ocean surrounding the Caribbean island of Bonaire

OVER HERE! Just as candy-cane-striped poles advertise barber shops, this crab's flashy legs help draw the attention of creatures who can form symbiotic relationships with the crab.

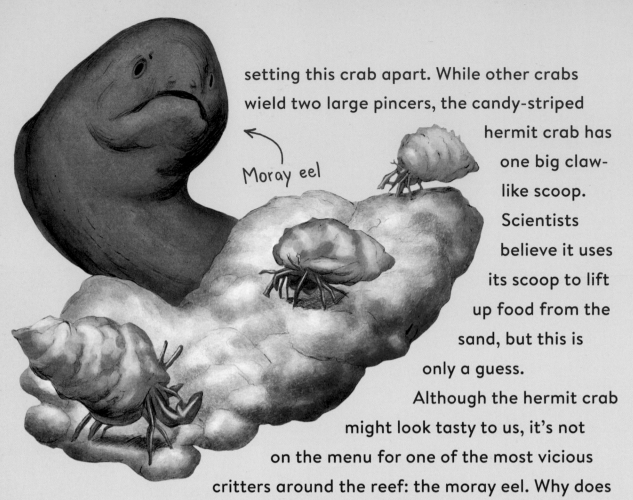

setting this crab apart. While other crabs wield two large pincers, the candy-striped

Moray eel

hermit crab has one big claw-like scoop. Scientists believe it uses its scoop to lift up food from the sand, but this is only a guess.

Although the hermit crab might look tasty to us, it's not on the menu for one of the most vicious critters around the reef: the moray eel. Why does the moray look the other way at all-you-can-eat candy crab legs? Scientists think the eel has a much better deal with the crabs: The crabs find all the mucus and other gross stuff growing on the eel's body to be quite tasty, and the eel enjoys being cleaned. It's a win-win!

"Deals" like this happen all the time in the natural world. When two kinds of organisms interact in a way that benefits both of them, scientists call their relationship **symbiotic**.

Leaves cookie-shaped holes in the flesh of its prey!

COOKIE-CUTTER SHARK

What do cookie cutters have in common with Isis, the Egyptian goddess of light? Well, not much . . . But they both inspired names for this small but sly shark!

The shark's genus name, *Isistius*, is a nod to Isis. Why the goddess of light? Well, the cookiecutter shark has **bioluminescent** organs called **photophores** on its side that give off greenish lights at night. Scientists can still only guess as to the function of these lights—perhaps they help the shark navigate the darkness of the deep oceans it calls home, or perhaps they confuse would-be predators.

The rest of its scientific name, *brasiliensis*, describes where the shark was first found by French scientists Jean René Constant Quoy and Joseph Paul Gaimard in the early nineteenth century—off the coast of Brazil.

A cookiecutter shark left several marks on this whale!

So how did a shark with a fancy name like *Isistius brasiliensis* end up being called the cookiecutter? It has to do with how these sharks eat. At night, they swim up near the surface of the ocean to take a bite out of unsuspecting sea creatures. Growing between 16 and 22 inches long, the cookiecutter shark is rather small, but that doesn't stop it from chomping on much larger prey—including giant squids!

The cookiecutter shark has special "suctorial lips" that allow it to attach itself to the sides of other fish. Once sufficiently suctioned to its prey, it inserts its super-sharp set of lower teeth through the prey's skin and drills through the flesh. (The cookiecutter shark has the largest teeth relative to its size of all sharks!) Then it gives its lower jaw a twist and pops out a plug of fish flesh in the shape of a tiny ice cream cone.

So why isn't it called the ice cream shark? Instead of being named after the shape of its bites, it's named for what it leaves behind: little holes resembling a sheet of cookie dough with cookies cut out of it. Yum!

SPECIES: *Isistius brasiliensis*

HABITAT: Oceans around the world, particularly tropical and temperate regions

SUBMARINE FOR DINNER?
Giant squids aren't the only oversize objects cookiecutter sharks munch on. They will also bite great white sharks and have even been known to try to eat nuclear submarines!

Flat as a pancake! →

PANCAKE TORTOISE

A tortoise, NOT a turtle! ←

True to its name, this tortoise is almost as flat as a pancake—a tiny pancake! These little guys grow to only about 6 inches long and weigh around 1 pound.

As a reptile with a shell, the pancake tortoise—also known as the African pancake tortoise—belongs to the Testudines order of turtles, terrapins, and tortoises. However, the pancake tortoise finds a way to stand out from the crowd. Unlike other members of the order Testudines, the pancake tortoise's shell has several openings between its plates, making it super lightweight and flexible. Thanks to this special adaptation, the pancake tortoise is the fastest of all tortoises—and this comes in handy when it needs to make a speedy getaway!

While other tortoises and turtles tuck into their shells when threatened by predators, the African pancake tortoise takes off running or climbs over rocks in order to escape. That's right—a climbing pancake tortoise. Has the world gone mad?

SPECIES: *Malacochersus tornieri*

HABITAT: Dry and rocky scrublands of Kenya and Tanzania

TURTLE OR TORTOISE? What's the main difference between a turtle and a tortoise? It's all about where they live: Tortoises spend their lives on land, while turtles spend most or all of their lives in water.

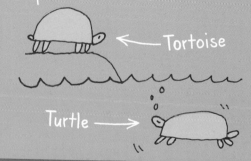

Tortoise

Turtle

Sometimes running and climbing aren't enough, though. In order to evade the mongooses and wild dogs that are hungry for pancakes, this tiny tortoise has adapted to become a hide-and-seek champion: The buttery yellow and syrupy brown coloration of its shell helps it camouflage itself among the rocks.

POTATO COD

A curious potato cod greets a diver.

SPECIES: *Epinephelus tukula*

HABITAT: Coral reefs in the Indian and Pacific Oceans

DID YOU KNOW? Some potato cod start out as females and turn into males later in life. The scientific term for an animal who goes through this transformation is **protogynous hermaphrodite.**

You've probably heard of fish-and-chips—it's a classic British meal. But have you ever heard of a fish that has its own chips?

Okay, *Epinephelus tukula* might not actually swim around with a basket of chips clutched in its fins, but it *is* covered in brown potato-shaped markings, hence its common name. And considering that potato cod grow as large as 6.5 feet long and can weigh over 220 pounds, if they *did* eat chips, they could probably eat a whole lot of them!

So what *do* they eat? The potato cod will feast on just about any fish that fits in its mouth, along with crabs, lobsters, octopuses, and whatever else it finds among the coral reefs. And "chew your food" is

102

one lesson the potato cod never learned—it often swallows its prey whole in just one gulp!

Fortunately, potato cod aren't interested in munching on humans. In fact, they are quite friendly to divers. Despite being territorial, they are naturally curious and have been observed nosing around divers and their equipment.

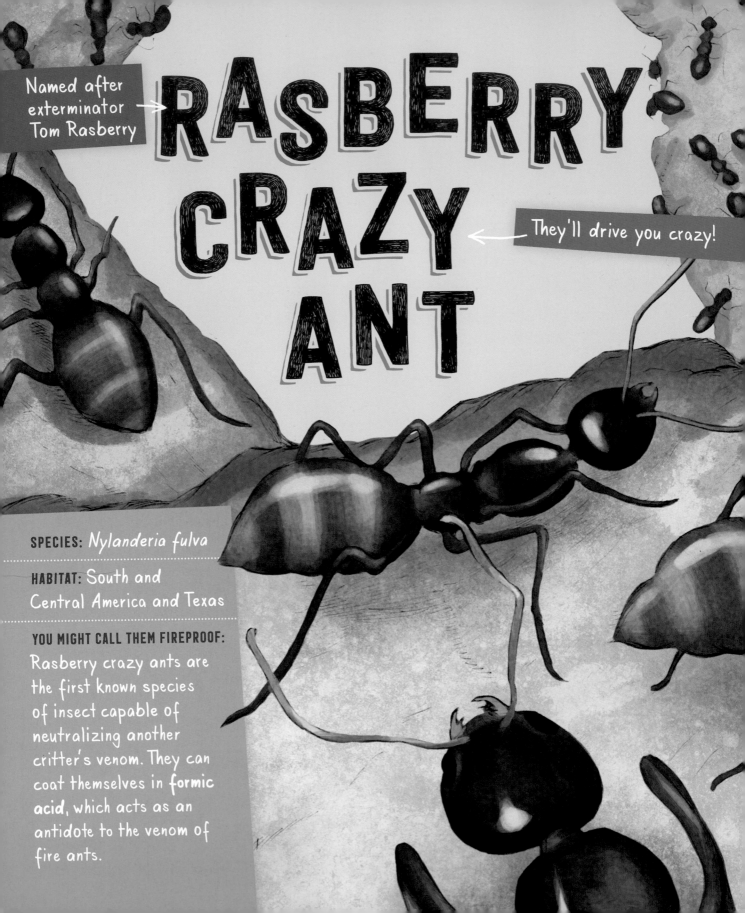

RASBERRY CRAZY ANT

Named after exterminator Tom Rasberry →

They'll drive you crazy! ←

SPECIES: *Nylanderia fulva*

HABITAT: South and Central America and Texas

YOU MIGHT CALL THEM FIREPROOF: Rasberry crazy ants are the first known species of insect capable of neutralizing another critter's venom. They can coat themselves in **formic acid**, which acts as an antidote to the venom of fire ants.

You might notice there is no "p" in the "Rasberry" in this ant's common name. It's not a misspelling! Their name might sound delicious when said aloud, but these ants aren't actually named after a berry—they're named after the man bent on destroying them.

Originally from South and Central America, Rasberry crazy ants—also known as tawny crazy ants—made the mistake of crossing into Texas, where they got more than a common name. They got a target placed on them.

Exterminator Tom Rasberry was the first to identify the ants, and he quickly got to work protecting the people of Texas from these six-legged nightmares. Rasberry made such a name for himself that NASA (the National Aeronautics and Space Administration) called him to save their mission control center in Houston from the ants!

Whether the "crazy" in their common name comes from their behavior or how they make people feel is up for debate. But this much is certain: *Nylanderia fulva* are tiny terrors. Instead of packing a powerfully painful bite like their cousin, the fire ant, Rasberry crazy ants drive people mad by invading homes in swarms, destroying electrical equipment, and reproducing seemingly quicker than they can be killed.

Don't believe us? Just ask Tom Rasberry. Despite claiming to have spent well over two thousand hours studying how to keep these crazies at bay, the exterminator remains stumped!

HONEY BADGER

Instead of being named for what they look like, these badgers are named for what they like to eat—honey! While honey badgers mostly eat reptiles, rodents, and insect **larvae**, they also love raiding beehives and feasting on honey.

The honey badger, also known as the ratel, belongs to the Mustelidae family of carnivores including badgers, weasels, ferrets, otters, and other animals. This particular member of the Mustelidae family is known for being a fierce fighter—but even though this is one bad badger, it doesn't go around looking for trouble. How could it? Its eyesight is as poor as its temperament is ferocious! Most of its scraps with other animals occur when would-be predators make the mistake of hunting the honey badger. Often, the badger is the only one walking away from these fights.

If a honey badger doesn't care to hang around and fight, it has a not-so-sweet way of making an escape. At the bottom of its tail are two stink glands similar to a skunk's that dribble out liquid stench bombs, giving the badger the chance to run (or dig) away. Maybe "rotten egg badger" would be a better name!

SPECIES: *Mellivora capensis*

HABITAT: *Africa and southwestern Asia*

BADGER BABIES: Honey badgers are born pink and hairless. It takes them about six months to grow to full size, but they don't develop the fighting and hunting skills they need to leave home (and their dear old ma) until they are at least a year old.

CHOCOLATE DIP DAMSELFISH

Looks like it was dipped in a bowl of chocolate!

One of the many species of damselfish

Who's ready for dessert?

The chocolate dip damselfish gets its common name from its two-tone body that is chocolatey brown up front and white in the back. It looks like a white fish that was dipped headfirst into a bowl of creamy chocolate. Talk about fondue!

SPECIES: *Chromis fieldi*

HABITAT: Coral reefs in the Indian Ocean, especially near Tanzania

CLOWNING AROUND: Damselfish belong to the Pomacentridae family of fish. It's a whopper of a family, consisting of 29 different genera and about 385 species of fish—including clown fish! (With all those clowns, the Pomacentridae family birthday parties must be out of this world.)

Not everyone agrees on this fish's common name—the chocolate dip damselfish is also known as the two-tone chromis or the two-tone damselfish—but whatever you call them, this much is certain: These tiny, tasty-sounding fish are quite feisty when other fish try to move in on

their territory,
especially once their
eggs have been laid! In
fact, it's the job of the
male damselfish to hang
around the eggs and protect
them until they hatch.

When they aren't laying eggs or
fighting off would-be intruders, chocolate dip
damselfish can be found hanging around coral reefs, dining
on zooplankton and other tiny underwater **invertebrates.**

MoRE SWEET

The chocolate dip damselfish, honey badger, and candy-striped hermit crab aren't the only animals that will have you reaching for a dessert menu. The scientists who named these next four creatures must have had sweets on the mind!

GELAE BEETLES
A genius name for a genus! Pronounced like "jelly," *gelae* is the first part of five food-themed scientific beetle names: *Gelae baen*, *Gelae belae*, *Gelae donut*, *Gelae fish*, and *Gelae rol*. Beetle discoverers Kelly B. Miller and Quentin D. Wheeler scooped the word "gelae" from the Latin word for "jellied," *gelatus*.

CHOCOLATE CHIP SEA STAR *(Protoreaster nodosus)*
This sea star might look like a cookie covered in chocolate chips, but those "chips" are actually horns that the sea star uses to deter predators. Best look elsewhere for a sweet treat!

ANIMALS

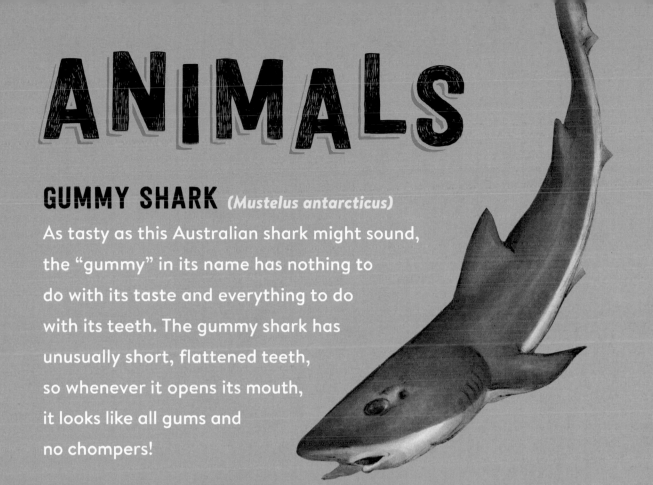

GUMMY SHARK *(Mustelus antarcticus)*

As tasty as this Australian shark might sound, the "gummy" in its name has nothing to do with its taste and everything to do with its teeth. The gummy shark has unusually short, flattened teeth, so whenever it opens its mouth, it looks like all gums and no chompers!

PINEAPPLE FISH *(Cleidopus gloriamaris)* With a body covered in yellow scales, this tiny, well-armored swimmer looks more than a little like a pineapple. And that's not it's only unique feature: When the pineapple fish opens its mouth, you can see the faint glow of **bioluminescent bacteria** living inside the **photophores** on the sides of its jaw.

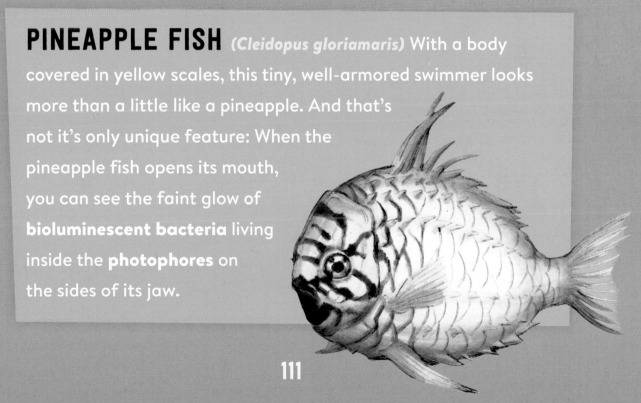

PIEZA PI

Say it out loud!

PIEZA KAKE

PIEZA PAN

PIEZA RHEA

PIEZA PI

When your scientific name is a reference to possibly the greatest food humans have ever created, who needs a common name?

The *Pieza pi* fly is just one species making up the *Pieza* genus of flies, which also includes *Pieza rhea* and *Pieza kake*. Beyond their delicious names, not much is known yet about the *Pieza* flies and the other members of the family Mythicomyiidae to which they belong. Although flies from this family are commonly found all over the world, they are teeny-tiny and incredibly little is known about any of them. That's got to be frustrating to scientists, no matter how you slice it!

The taxonomical genius behind the *Pieza* names is scientist Neal Evenhuis, who must have been hungry for a pizza party when he discovered this fly. If there was a Taxonomy Hall of Fame, Evenhuis would have to be among its first admissions. With more than five hundred species names to his credit, you can probably understand why he's prone to getting creative with words!

In an interview with the *New York Times*, Evenhuis was asked how many recently discovered species of animals are still waiting to be assigned names. "There are not enough taxonomists to go around," he said. So what are you waiting for? It's time to get naming!

SPECIES: *Pieza pi*

HABITAT: Found all around the world

I YAM WHAT I YAM: In addition to his *Pieza* flies, Evenhuis named a species of carnivorous fly *Campsicnemus popeye* because its bulging front legs reminded him of the famed cartoon spinach-eater's muscular arms.

BANANA SLUG

One of the largest slugs in North America

Don't try to peel this banana!

114

magine you are walking through the moist redwood forests of the U.S. Pacific Northwest and you suddenly see a banana on the ground . . . and it's moving! You might think you're losing your mind, but relax—you're only staring at a banana slug.

The "banana" in its name comes from the shape of its body and its yellow coloration, although the banana slug can also be green (like unripe bananas) or white (like a banana on the inside) depending on its diet and environment.

Just how big are these bananas? The largest banana slugs grow almost 10 inches long and weigh a tad over 4 ounces, making this slug one of the largest in North America (although the banana slug looks like a slacker compared to the world's largest air-breathing land slug, the *Limax cinereoniger*, which can be found sliming through the forests of Europe).

To get around, the banana slug uses its one and only foot, perfectly placed on its belly, to propel itself forward, sliding along the slime it oozes out of its body.

GENUS: *Ariolimax*

HABITAT: Forests along the west coast of North America

FIGHT! WIN! SLUG! The banana slug is the official mascot for the University of California–Santa Cruz. Go banana slugs!

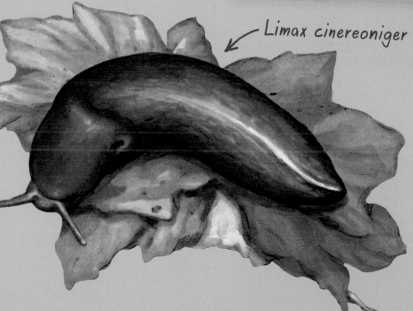

← *Limax cinereoniger*

Too cool to split in a rush, the banana slug also uses its slime as a defense against predators. Anything that tries to make a meal out of this banana instantly spits it out and gets a numb mouth thanks to the special chemistry of the slime—although this has not stopped clever raccoons from rolling banana slugs in dirt to cover up their slime and make them safe to eat!

In addition to its single foot, the banana slug has two sets of feelers on its head. It uses the top feelers to detect light and the bottom feelers to smell. It can retract the feelers back into its head and even can grow them back if they are damaged.

5

JUST PLAIN WEIRD NAMES ???

By now, you might be wondering, "Do scientists ever run out of weird names to give the animals they discover?" Well, you better buckle up, because this might be the last chapter, but we're just getting started when it comes to "weird." From the **BIRDBEAK DOGFISH** to the **WHITE-BELLIED GO-AWAY BIRD** to the **AYE-AYE**, the animal names in this chapter will make you scratch your head and think "What on earth?!"

Even the extreme weirdness of the names won't fully prepare you for some of the wacky behaviors and characteristics these animals exhibit. You're about to meet giant rats, hissing cockroaches, a shark that looks like a shaggy carpet, and one of the ocean's most baffling inhabitants: the **HEADLESS CHICKEN MONSTER**. Get ready to get weird!

RED-LIPPED BATFISH

Has gorgeous red lips

A bat-shaped body

If you've ever dreamed of kissing a fish, it's time to pucker up! When viewed from overhead, the red-lipped batfish's shape— a wide, boxy upper body tapering down to a tiny tail—resembles a bat. But it's those lips that really catch the eye. That's right this particular member of the Ogcocephalidae family of batfish has large, pouty red lips that make it look like it's wearing lipstick underwater! While we don't know for sure *why* these batfish have red lips, some scientists think the bright color helps attract mates.

The red-lipped batfish definitely isn't afraid to stand out. Not only does it sport the finest lips under the sea, it also has a unique way of getting around: It uses its specially adapted pectoral fins to walk across the seafloor instead of swimming.

Fortunately, this fish doesn't have to walk too fast to catch food. Instead, the food comes to the batfish! The red-lipped batfish has a strange structure on its head called an **illicium,** which operates like a tiny fishing rod complete with "bait" to lure other fish over to take a bite . . . But soon enough they discover it's the last bite they will ever take!

The last part of its specific name, *darwini,* is a reference to renowned naturalist Charles Darwin, who studied several kinds of animals in and around the Galapagos Islands where the red-lipped batfish is found.

SPECIES: *Ogcocephalus darwini*

HABITAT: Galapagos Islands

BUTT PROPELLER: As if those lips aren't strange enough, take a look the batfish's backside: It sports an anal fin that looks like a propeller!

The animal-who-must-not-be-named? With a face stuck in a constant state of shock, this terrifying-looking critter who haunts the forests of Madagascar is so strange that locals have long believed it to possess magic—dangerous magic!

Well-known animal discoverer George Shaw tried to hang the name "long-fingered lemur" on this nasty of the night, but it never took. "Aye-aye" is believed to have derived from the Malagasy phrase "heh heh" meaning "I don't know." Locals are convinced that this creature is bad luck, so when asked to say its name, they simply answer, "Aye-aye" ("I don't know").

It's easy to see why some think the aye-aye is magical—after all, it lives its life in mystery, sleeping away its days curled in a nest of balled-up leaves way up high in the branches of the Madagascan rain forest. Aye-ayes come out only at night and rarely reach the ground.

Plus, they even have a "magical" power. Aye-ayes are believed to use a technique called **percussive foraging** when searching for food. By thumping their long middle fingers on trees, aye-ayes can determine whether there is food beneath the bark. If you are an insect larva living inside a tree in Madagascar, the aye-aye truly is a nightmare!

SPECIES: *Doubentonia madagascariensis*

HABITAT: Madagascar

HEY, COUSIN! Aye-ayes belong to the order primates, which includes apes, chimpanzees . . . and you! That's right—humans share an order with aye-ayes.

Aye-ayes use their long middle fingers to search for food.

121

ODD ANIMALS OF

I f you're looking for some of the world's wackiest—and wackiest-named—animals, look no further than Madagascar. The African island is packed with incredible biodiversity, and many of the animals on the island are found there and nowhere else.

GIANT JUMPING RAT (*Hypogeomys antimena*) Rabbits are found almost everywhere on earth, but not on Madagascar. The island is home to a hopper, though—the giant jumping rat. This creature sports long pointed ears and large rear legs and feet, just like a rabbit, and it might even best a rabbit in a high jump contest: The giant jumping rat can jump 40 inches straight up in the air!

MADAGASCAR HISSING COCKROACH

(*Gromphadorhina portentosa*) Madagascar hissing cockroaches can make a hissing sound by expelling air out through their **spiracles** (breathing pores that operate a bit like blowholes). They're fighters, too: The male roach has two horns on top of his head, which he uses to ram other males to establish dominance during the mating season.

MADAGASCAR

SATANIC LEAF-TAILED GECKO

(*Uroplatus phantasticus*) These critters look more like dried-up leaves than geckos, and to complete the ruse, they often hang from branches alongside actual leaves. If a predator manages to see through the disguise, however, these little devils open their mouths wide, showing off a bright red mouth, and scream! Their satanic moniker comes from their red eyes and the horn on top of their head.

ELEPHANT BIRD (family Aepyornithidae)

The now-extinct elephant bird just might be the most incredible bird you've never seen. Standing up to 10 feet tall and weighing more than 1,700 pounds, it's easy to understand how this bird earned the "elephant" in its name—in fact, it was one of the largest birds of all time. And unlike a lot of giant animals that once roamed the earth, the elephant bird isn't prehistoric—in fact, it went extinct only about one thousand years ago!

123

BIRDBEAK DOGFISH

Has a pointed, beak-like snout

Hunts in packs

T hanks to its long, beak-like snout that narrows toward the tip like a shovel and its low-lying **dorsal fins**, this dogfish shark is sometimes called a shovelnose spiny dogfish along with its most common name, birdbeak dogfish.

Whatever you call it, this 4-foot-long shark can be found swimming all over the Pacific and Atlantic Oceans at depths of 1,300 to 4,600 feet. Unlike many other members of the Squaliformes order, the birdbeak trawls the deep ocean without the snazzy use of **bioluminescence**.

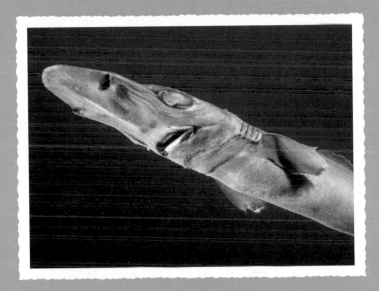

Fortunately, though, this dog can hunt! Skimming closely over ocean floors, it fetches crabs, lobsters, and whatever fish it can find. The "dog" in "dogfish" refers to its hunting habits: Like other members of the Squalidae family, all commonly called dogfish, the birdbeak hunts in packs like wild dogs.

Unlike dogs, all sharks in the dogfish family have dorsal fins equipped with venomous spines. Not quite sharks with laser beams, but still pretty wicked!

125

SPECIES: *Deania calcea*

HABITAT: Deep in the Pacific and Atlantic Oceans

SHARK PUPPIES: When giving birth, birdbeak dogfish can have up to twelve baby sharks, known as "pups."

Looks like a tasseled rug!

TASSELED WOBBEGONG

Means "shaggy beard"

The word *wobbegong* comes from an Australian Aboriginal language and means "shaggy beard." And it's easy to see how this strange shark got its name—just look at all of that hair around its face and mouth!

But actually, it's not hair at all. Instead, the wobbegong is covered in hundreds of tiny tassel-like **barbels** that twist in the water, helping this 4-foot-long creature blend in with its colorful coral reef surroundings.

126

Barbels aren't just for camouflage, though: These slim sensory organs contain special taste buds that wobbegongs—and other fish with barbels, like carp and catfish—use to search for food.

SPECIES: *Eucrossorhinus dasypogon*

HABITAT: The coral reefs around Indonesia and Australia

HUNGRY CARPETS: Tasseled wobbegong have been observed eating sharks almost 80 percent their size!

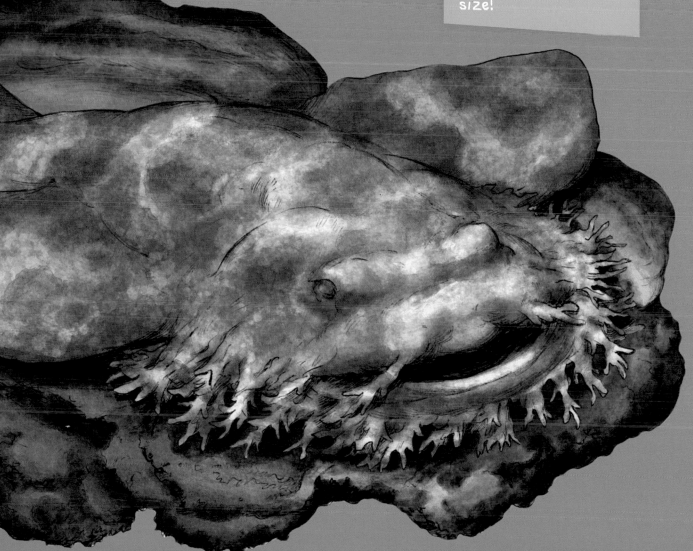

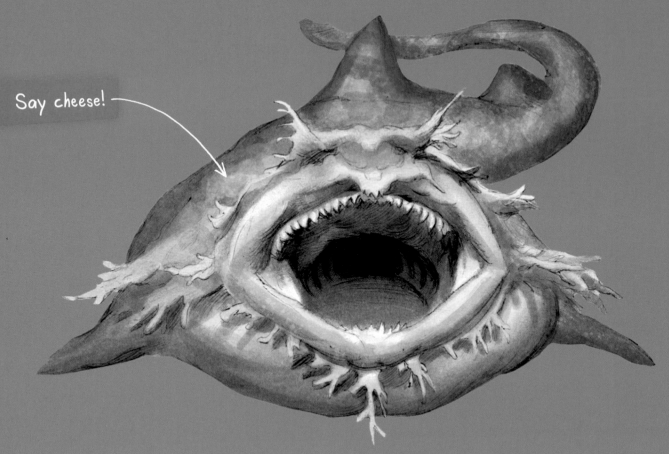

Say cheese!

The wobbegong's patterns and "tassels" might remind you of a rug—so it makes sense that this creature belongs to an order of sharks commonly called carpet sharks. And like a carpet, the wobbegong spends its time close to shallow seafloors, moving as little as possible.

At night, the wobbegong ventures to the edges of reefs, where it lies motionless and patiently waits for prey to swim by. Once it spots dinner, the wobbegong plays a sneaky trick: It wiggles its tail so the tip looks like a small fish, which lures real fish closer. Then, with some of the strongest jaws of all sharks, this "carpet" takes a bite and it's curtains for the prey!

WAXY MONKEY TREE FROG

Secretes its own sunblock

Grips branches with monkey-like hands

Lives high up in the trees

If you spent all day every day lounging around in the hot sun, you would need some serious sunscreen. Ah, but wouldn't it be nice if your skin could produce its own sunscreen, so you wouldn't have to keep putting it on?

Well, if you were the waxy monkey tree frog, you would be able to do just that. This curious little frog secretes a chemical concoction that acts as sunblock, protecting it from the sun's harmful rays—and giving it a waxy glow!

A waxy monkey tree frog spreading its "sunblock"

SPECIES: *Phyllomedusa sauvagii*

HABITAT: South America's forested Chaco region

DON'T MISS A SPOT! The waxy monkey tree frog's flexible legs can reach all over its body, allowing it to spread its "sunblock" to those hard-to-reach spots.

So, the "waxy" part is all fine and dandy, but what about the rest of this frog's wacky name? Well, like other tree frog species, the waxy monkey lives life high up in the treetops at the upper limits of the forest. Remarkably, it has monkey-like hands that can grasp, and these come in very handy when it comes time to move between the trees: Instead of hopping along branches like a normal frog, the waxy monkey tree frog uses its hands to walk from branch to branch.

Those trees aren't just for monkeying around, though. They play an important role in how the waxy monkey reproduces: The frogs lay their eggs in the leaves of trees overhanging lakes and ponds. This way, when the tadpoles hatch, they slide right down into a welcoming body of water where they can begin the first phase of their frog lives.

CHICKEN TURTLE

Tastes like chicken (really!)

f this creature's common name conjures up Images of a chicken-turtle hybrid, you might be disappointed to find out that the chicken turtle is all turtle. But they do taste like chicken! At least, that's how people described them when turtle soup was more commonly eaten in the United States, a trend that slowed in the mid-twentieth century.

The chicken turtle sometimes goes by another common name: American snake neck. Why? Its head and neck are more than three-fourths as long as its **carapace**, which is what scientists call a turtle's shell. With that long neck sticking up, it's easy to see its resemblance to a snake!

Since demand for turtle soup has gone down, these turtles are free to do the eating themselves—and they'll eat just about anything. Fruit, plants, fish, frogs, or insects? It's all on the menu! These omnivores aren't particular when it comes to food.

They *are* pretty particular when it comes to temperature, though—at least while they are still eggs. In fact, the soil where chicken turtle eggs incubate determines the sex of the future turtles. When the temperature is around 77°F (25°C), most of the offspring will turn out to be males, while temperatures closer to 86°F (30°C) will produce mostly females.

SPECIES: *Deirochelys reticularia*

HABITAT: The wetlands of the southeastern United States, from Florida up to North Carolina

THAT'S JUST CONFUSING! The chicken turtle isn't the only animal named after another animal—there are also sea lions, fox squirrels, leopard frogs, scorpion flies, and skunk bears, to name just a few.

DOGFACE BUTTERFLY

Wing pattern looks like a pooch!

Can you spot the dog silhouette?

SPECIES: *Zerene eurydice*

HABITAT: California

SENSITIVE SETAE: Like other butterflies, the dogface has special "hairs" called **setae** on its body. Setae help butterflies sense vibrations in the air, allowing them to navigate their surroundings.

What is the first state to have a state insect? California! What insect did they choose? The dogface butterfly! Maybe the dogface butterfly was chosen because it is **endemic** (native) to California. Or maybe it was those pesky kids . . .

Fourth graders at Daily Elementary School in Fresno, California, suggested that California adopt the dogface butterfly as its state insect by submitting their idea to the state legislature in 1972. And it worked—today, an image of the dogface butterfly can be found on California driver's licenses below the driver's signature.

A dogface butterfly in a cocoon

That's how the dogface got its fame, but where did it get its name? Well, if you take a close look at the male butterfly's wings, you will see a silhouette of what appears to be a dog's face. Many people think it looks like a standard poodle. What kind of pooch does it look like to you?

The dogface butterfly may have an unusual name, but they live just like other butterflies—they start out as caterpillars, create cocoons, and then break through as butterflies and feast on the nectar of flowers.

If only dogface caterpillars were called "puppies" before they crawled into their cocoon!

HEADLESS CHICKEN MONSTER

Resembles a chicken with its head cut off →

→ Only *looks* like a monster!

Deep in the dark waters of the Southern Ocean surrounding Antarctica swims a headless chicken monster. But not to fear— this monster is really just a cucumber . . . a sea cucumber, that is! Sea cucumbers are marine animals related to starfish and sea urchins. Many of them have cucumber-shaped bodies, hence their name, and they can be found on seafloors around the world.

So how did a sea cucumber wind up with such a monstrous moniker? Well, this particular cucumber looks a bit like a chicken that's about to go into the oven! Fortunately, though, this "monster" isn't exactly the stuff of

SPECIES: *Enypniastes eximia*

HABITAT: While sea cucumbers live on seafloors around the world, so far the headless chicken monster has been spotted only in the Southern Ocean and the Gulf of Mexico.

THE DIGESTION SHOW: Since the headless chicken monster's body is more or less transparent, you can watch as the food it eats passes through its body. Gross! Or . . . cool?

136

nightmares—it's fairly small, between 4 and 10 inches long, with a reddish-pink coloration.

Very little is known about the headless chicken monster, including how many of these "monsters" exist, but we do know this: Unlike most sea cucumbers, this headless chicken of the sea has fins, which allow it to scurry away from predators. In fact, the headless chicken monster's frilly fins have earned it another, much less frightening common name—the Spanish dancer! The headless chicken monster also has clusters of tentacles that help it move and gather grub.

WHITE-BELLIED GO-AWAY BIRD

Look at that soft white belly!

The sound of its call

As you travel through the acacia savannas of East Africa, you hear someone calling "go away!" You look around, but there's no one in sight. Suddenly, you notice a gray, white-bellied bird scurrying like a squirrel from branch to branch in an acacia tree. The bird stops and cries out again: "Go away!"

This bird's common name is a combination of how it looks and how it sounds. It has a bright-white belly, and its call sounds an awful lot like someone saying, "Go away!" Even if it isn't *actually* telling you to go away, its call can be so annoying that you might just leave the scene anyway.

SPECIES: *Corythaixoides leucogaster*

HABITAT: The woodlands, savannas, and acacia steppes of East Africa

YOUR TURN! Give a familiar animal a new common name based on the sound it makes. What if, instead of cats and dogs, we called our household pets meows and barks?

But its call is not annoying to all. Many of the birds who live alongside the white-bellied go-away bird in central and southern Africa appreciate its cry, which serves as a warning that potential predators like leopards, snakes, and monkeys are nearby.

When it isn't escaping predators, the white-bellied go-away bird enjoys feasting on fruit, seeds, nectar, leaves, and small **invertebrates.** It can often be found in wooded areas, high up in the trees, but also forays into the acacia steppes and savannas to eat the green pods of the acacia tree.

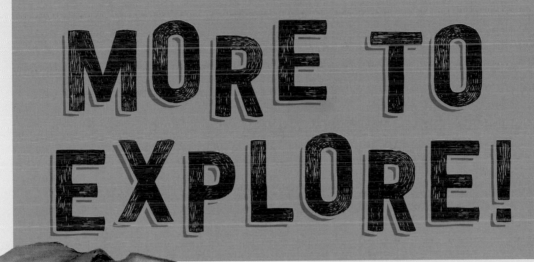

MORE TO EXPLORE!

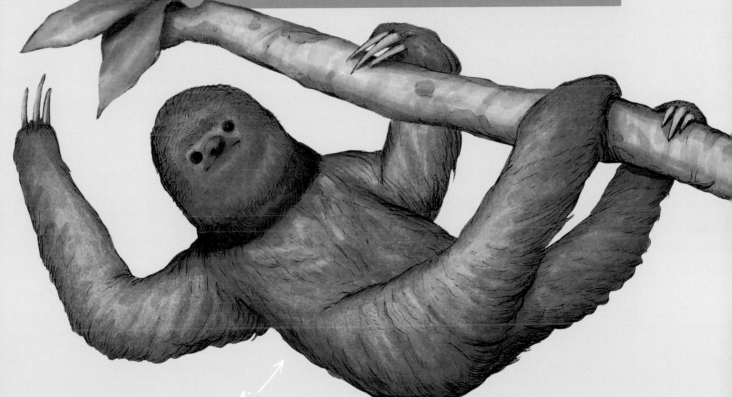

AND THE AWARD GOES TO...

If you thought we had run out of curiously named animals, think again! The world is full of amazing creatures with equally amazing names, and new species are being discovered and classified all the time. These next few critters deserve honorable mentions for their truly special names.

LONGEST SCIENTIFIC NAME: *Parastratiosphecomyia stratiosphecomyioides*

Despite its incredibly long name, this specimen is actually just a small fly. Its genus name means "near soldier wasp-fly," while its species name means "wasp fly–like." Put it together and you get "near soldier wasp-fly wasp fly–like," which is an equally long—and confusing—name!

SHORTEST COMMON NAME: Ai *(Bradypus torquatus)*

Also known as the maned sloth, the ai is one of four known species of three-toed sloths and can be found only in Brazil.

MOST HEAD-SCRATCHING NAME: Elephant Mosquito *(Toxorhynchites rutilus)*

How did something as small as a mosquito get named after something as enormous as an elephant? Well, with a body of about an inch long, the elephant mosquito is one of the biggest mosquitoes in the world!

COZIEST NAME: Cashmere Goat *(Capra aegagrus hircus)*
While cashmere is prized among humans as one of the softest
fabrics to wear, cashmere goats just grow the stuff all over their
bellies to stay warm.

**MOST MADE-UP SOUNDING
NAME: Zebroid** *(Equus zebra
and Equus caballus)* What do you
get when you cross a zebra with a horse
or a donkey? A zebroid, of course! These
hybrid creatures are also called zedonks,
zorses, or zonkeys.

MOST LIKELY TO CHANGE NAMES: Mimic Octopus
(Thaumoctopus mimicus) The mimic octopus can radically change
its appearance to look like a variety of other sea creatures. It might
need some new names to go with all those disguises!

MOST OBVIOUS NAME: Anteater **(suborder Vermilingua)**
Quick—guess what an anteater eats!

MOST FLOWERY NAME: Flower-Faced Bat *(Anthops
ornatus)* One of the few things known about this small bloodsucker
is that its yellowish-orange nose resembles a flower. Still no word
on how it smells, though . . .

HOW TO
DISCOVER
AND NAME
AN ORGANISM

While most mammals have already been identified and named, scientists estimate that there are still millions of species—especially fish and insects—yet to be discovered. Maybe you will be the one to make the next great animal discovery! On the right page are a few tips for how to find and classify an organism. But first things first:

Make sure a friendly adult joins you on any animal-seeking expeditions. And don't do anything dangerous in the wild! Good scientists are adventurous, but they use common sense, too, especially when interacting with new species.

1 **DISCOVER** a creature you have never seen before. You can do this anywhere—around your home, at a park, or at the school playground.

2 **OBSERVE** the animal. Don't touch or disturb it. Instead, keep a safe distance and jot down some notes about what it looks like. You might take a picture of it or draw it.

3 **RESEARCH** to find out if your "discovery" has already been discovered. Try to match your creature with an existing organism online or in animal books in your local library. You can ask teachers or librarians to help you with this.

Crabs

4 If you can't find any record of your creature anywhere, then you might have a new species on your hands! It's time to **NAME IT** and **DESCRIBE IT**. Give it a scientific and common name and write a detailed description of it.

5 **SPREAD THE WORD!** You might try publishing information about your discovery so that scientists in the field can read and react to it. A professor at a local university who has experience publishing articles may be able to help you with this. Or you could share your discovery online (with your parents' or guardians' permission). These days, many scientists share information on social media!

6 To have your discovery formally recognized as a new species, submit an application to the **International Commission on Zoological Nomenclature** (iczn.org).

WEIRD AND WILD NAME GENERATOR

So you've just discovered a new animal! What are you going to call it? There are so many possibilities and it's hard to know where to start. But not to fear! The Wild and Wacky Name Generator is here to help.

Choose one word from each column that best describes the animal, then combine them to form a name. Even more fun: Choose a crazy combination of words and then draw what an animal with that name might look like! (The bedazzled spitting volcano cow would be a sight to behold . . .)

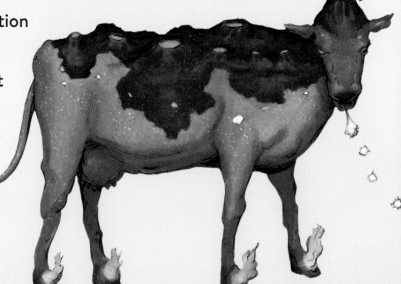

APPEARANCE	BEHAVIOR	HABITAT	TYPE OF ANIMAL
leafy	dancing	cave	bug
spotted	howling	swamp	fish
striped	spitting	water	frog
flaming	smiling	treetop	bird
hairy	groaning	mountain	rodent
spiny	jumping	desert	lizard
wrinkly	digging	polar	monkey
speckled	racing	backyard	pig
sparkling	creeping	sea	worm
headless	snapping	savanna	slug
frilly	slithering	rain forest	cat
waxy	crawling	volcano	dog
tiny	vanishing	grass	cow
humongous	sneaking	sky	horse
blobby	farting	pond	shark
bedazzled	hiding	river	sponge
scaly	hibernating	lake	ghost
angelic	flying	snow	dragon
spooky	spinning	dirt	beast
fancy	snoozing	galactic	monster

GLOSSARY

AMPHIPODA: An order of small invertebrate animals, found in aquatic and coastal environments; falls within the Arthropoda phylum.

APOSEMATIC: An aposematic animal has a bright coloration indicating it is poisonous, which discourages predators.

ARTHROPODA: A phylum of small invertebrate animals with segmented bodies, jointed appendages, and an exoskeleton, including insects and crustaceans.

BACTERIA: A domain of single-cell microorganisms that have cell walls but no organized nucleus. While some bacteria can make you sick, others are used in vaccines and antibiotics to prevent and cure illnesses.

BARBEL: A tassel-like fleshy filament found on some fish.

BELL: The dome-shaped top of a jellyfish.

BINOMIAL NOMENCLATURE: The two-term naming system developed by Carl Linnaeus that is used to create scientific names.

BIOLUMINESCENCE: The process by which an animal produces light from its body.

BROOD POUCH: A small pouch that animals like frogs, fish, seahorses, and seadragons use to carry and protect their eggs before they hatch.

BURROW: A hole that an animal digs and lives in.

BUSH: An Australian term for rural, forested land.

CARAPACE: The top shell of a turtle. A turtle's bottom shell, which protects its insides from the ground, is called a plastron.

CARUNCLE: Brightly colored, lumpy pieces of flesh that hang around the ears, eyes, throats, and necks of certain animals, especially birds like chickens and turkeys.

CEPHALOPODS: Animals that belong to the Cephalopoda class of marine creatures, including octopuses, nautiluses, and squids.

CHROMATOPHORES: Cells found in certain animals that allow the animal to change its coloring.

CIRRI: Thin, hair-like structures found on some sea creatures, including the sarcastic fringehead.

COASTAL SHELF OR CONTINENTAL SHELF: The portion of a continent that extends into shallow sea water. An abundance of ocean life can often be found on coastal shelves.

COMMON NAME: The name by which an animal species is commonly referred to.

CONGLOBATION: The process by which something, like a pill bug, takes the shape of a ball.

CRITICALLY ENDANGERED SPECIES: A species with a low population in the wild that is at risk of extinction.

CRUSTACEA: The subphylum of animals that includes shrimp, lobsters, and crabs. These animals are known as crustaceans.

CRYPSIS: An animal's ability to avoid detection by other animals (a chameleon's ability to change color is one example of crypsis).

DORSAL FIN: The fin on a fish's back.

ENDEMIC: Found in a specific place (the aye-aye is endemic to Madagascar, for example).

ENTOMOLOGIST: A scientist who studies insects.

EUKARYA: A domain of organisms with a nucleus in their cells. This domain includes all the animals in the world—including you!

EXOSKELETON: A skeletal structure on the outside of an animal (instead of the inside, like humans).

FORMIC ACID: A naturally occurring chemical found in some ants, which can be weaponized as a venom spray.

GENE: A unit of DNA that carries genetic information from parent to offspring and determines which characteristics the offspring will inherit.

GOLDILOCKS ZONE: A tiny area where heat spewing from hydrothermal vents mixes with cold water to create a climate perfect for certain kinds of marine life.

HYALURONAN: A chemical found in high abundance in naked mole rats. Scientists believe the quantity of hyaluronan in naked mole rats protects them from cancer. The chemical is also found in human bodies, but not in high enough quantities to offer the same protection.

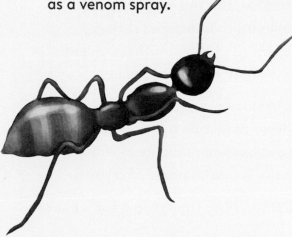

HYDROTHERMAL VENT: An opening in the seafloor through which hot water from below the Earth's crust flows out.

ILLICIUM: A structure on the heads of anglerfish (like the red-lipped batfish) that lures prey.

INDO-PACIFIC: A region of Earth's seas including the tropical Indian Ocean waters and the western and central Pacific Ocean waters.

INSECTIVORE: A plant or animal that eats insects.

INTERNATIONAL COMMISSION ON ZOOLOGICAL NOMENCLATURE: The international governing body of scientific names for animals.

INVERTEBRATES: Animals without backbones.

JOEY: An Australian term for a young animal, especially a kangaroo or wombat.

KLEPTOPARASITIC: A type of feeding behavior practiced by some animals in which they routinely eat what other animals caught, killed, or prepared.

LARVAE: The worm-like babies of many insect species.

LIVING FOSSIL: An animal that has remained mostly unchanged since previous geological eras. Often its relatives are extinct.

MALACOLOGIST: A scientist who specializes in studying mollusks.

MANDIBLES: The jawbones of a fish, mammal, or insect.

MARINE SNOW: Bits of organic material that drift down to the ocean depths.

MARSUPIAL: A mammal, such as a kangaroo or wombat, that carries its young in a pouch.

MOLLUSKS: Invertebrates with soft bodies belonging to the phylum Mollusca.

NERITIC ZONE: The part of the ocean close to the shore. It is home to abundant amounts of marine life.

NOCTURNAL: Describes an animal that is active at night and sleeps during the day.

ORGANISM: An individual life form.

PARASITES: Organisms that survive by stealing resources from other organisms.

PARASITOIDS: Organisms that begin as larvae and consume another life (their "host") in order to grow into a mature adult.

PATAGIUM: A flying dragon's wing.

PERCUSSIVE FORAGING: The method by which an aye-aye thumps its finger on trees to determine if there's food beneath the bark.

PHOTOPHORE: A light-producing organ found in many sea creatures.

PISCIVOROUS: Describes an animal that feeds on fish.

PROTOGYNOUS HERMAPHRODITE: An animal that begins life as a female and later becomes male.

PUPA: An insect in the stage of development between being a larva and being an adult.

ROSTRAL PROTUBERANCE: A bump sticking out of the front end of an animal, usually around the mouth or nose.

SCIENTIFIC NAME: The formal two-part name scientists use to refer to a species. Scientific names are based on Latin grammatical forms and written in *italics*.

SCULPIN: A type of fish from the order Scorpaeniformes known for living on the ocean floor.

SCUTE: A type of plate found in the armor or shells of certain creatures like armadillos and turtles.

SETAE: Stiff, bristly, hairlike structures covering some animals.

SEXUAL DIMORPHISM: A condition where the male and female specimens of a single species are very different in terms of size or appearance.

SLINGSHOT FEEDING: A goblin shark's method of thrusting its mouth forward several inches to grab prey.

SPIRACLES: External openings in animals that help them breathe. They can be found in some fish, a lot of insects, and certain spiders.

SPINNERET: Organ used by spiders and silkworms to produce silk.

SYMBIOTIC RELATIONSHIP: A long-term relationship between different species in which their interactions benefit each other.

TAXONOMY: The science of defining and classifying organisms based on what they have in common with each other. Scientists who practice taxonomy are called taxonomists.

FURTHER READING

For more information about the animals featured in this book—and many other animals and amazing nature facts!—check out the following organizations. You can also ask the teachers and librarians at your school and local library to help you find books and additional resources on specific animals.

THE SMITHSONIAN (*smithsonianmag.com/science-nature/wildlife*)

NATIONAL GEOGRAPHIC (*kids.nationalgeographic.com*)

OCEANA (*oceana.org/marine-life*)

CURIOUS TAXONOMY (*curioustaxonomy.net*)

ASSOCIATION OF ZOOS AND AQUARIUMS (*aza.org*)

A NOTE ON CONSERVATION

Many of the magnificent animals featured in this book, including those on the opposite page, are endangered or vulnerable to extinction. Fortunately, there are organizations working to save endangered species. For more information, check out these resources:

The Wildlife Conservation Society (wcs.org) is on a mission to save "wildlife and wild places worldwide through science, conservation action, and inspiring people to value nature." The WCS protects 200 million square miles of wild places around the world through some 500 projects in over 60 countries.

The Sierra Club (sierraclub.org) is one of the oldest and largest environmental organizations in the United States. It provides several ways for people to get involved with conservation, including volunteering opportunities.

The Nature Conservancy (nature.org) is a global organization on a mission to create a world where people and nature can thrive. It uses the combined power of more than one million members and over 400 scientists to conserve natural resources.

The National Wildlife Federation (nwf.org) is the largest private nonprofit conservation organization in the United States. The NWF focuses on education and advocacy in its mission to increase fish and wildlife populations, and it offers programming for young people.

If you live in the United States, you might also research your state government's department of conservation and see if there are any ways for young people to get involved with wildlife protection.

AYE-AYE

RED-LIPPED BATFISH

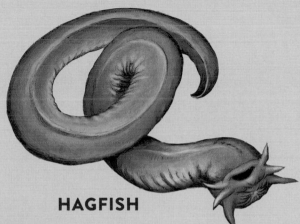

HAGFISH

PANCAKE TORTOISE

BIRDBEAK DOGFISH

BA HUMBUGI

ABOUT THE AUTHORS:

MATTHEW MURRIE is a former public high school teacher, curriculum writer, and private academy instructor. His father, **STEVE MURRIE**, is a retired science teacher. Matthew and Steve are the coauthors of several books for young readers.

ABOUT THE ILLUSTRATOR:

JULIE BENBASSAT is an illustrator living in Brooklyn, NY. A recent graduate of the Rhode Island School of Design, she strives to infuse aspects from the natural world into her work whenever she can.

PHOTO CREDITS: